SOCIAL SKILLS SOLUTIONS

A Hands-on Manual for Teaching Social Skills to Children with Autism

Written and developed by:

Kelly McKinnon, M.A., BCBA

Janis Krempa, M.Ed., BCBA

SOCIAL SKILLS SOLUTIONS
A Hands-on Manual for Teaching Social Skills to Children with Autism

Copyright © 2002 Janis Krempa, M.Ed. BCBA
              Kelly McKinnon, M.A. BCBA

Published by: DRL Books, Inc.
               37 East 18th Street
               10th Floor
               New York, New York 10003
               Phone: 800-853-1057
                       212-604-9637
               Fax: 212-206-9329
               www.drlbooks.com

Editor: Kimberly Fusco
Art Director: Judy Law
Art Assistant: Michi Dundon

Library of Congress number: 2004108822
ISBN number: 978-0-9665266-9-1

Part 1: GETTING STARTED

TABLE OF CONTENTS

PART 2 GETTING TO WORK

FOREWORD

At a time when news reports confirm the long held suspicion of clinicians and educators about increases in the prevalence of children being classified as falling in the Pervasive Developmental Disorder spectrum, additions such as this manual to the armamentarium of tools to address their challenges are highly welcome. The years of combined experience of Ms. Krempa and Mrs. McKinnon teaching children in the autism spectrum has resulted in an excellent and comprehensive step-by-step guide for the teaching of social skills. Their work is particularly helpful at this time in which the added effect of early identification and intensive intervention can often result in better outcomes. As a result, cohorts of children acquire basic functional, communicative, and academic skills allowing them to participate in mainstream instruction and regular activities, but they remain less effective in the establishment and sustainment of stable relationships and in need of significant growth in their social proficiency. Given the recognized need in all of us for a social network, small as it might be, providing these children with the tools to form their own is an invaluable contribution.

At the basis of the work produced by Ms. McKinnon and Ms. Krempa for this book is a necessary and well-researched understanding of the social skills literature. Their dense bibliography and their constant reference to additional citations to supply the interested reader with complementary sources to their work speak of their facility and knowledge of this literature. Their extensive read of this area along with their direct clinical experience make the theoretical blend into the practical, obtaining their expressed desire throughout the book to make this a functional endeavor for children affected with social deficits.

The selection of methodology, namely applied behavior analysis, which is backed in the autism literature as the intervention of choice for children in the autism spectrum, is another point of strength in Ms. Krempa and Ms. McKinnon's social skills program. Although misinformation about the use of this methodology has in some instances led to erroneous conclusions, such as the belief that children taught with this approach cannot use their newly gained skills appropriately in practical situations, the fact remains that, as any other area of human behavior, social functioning can be addressed by breaking it down to its smallest components and subsequently generalizing the achieved mastery over independent skills to increasingly novel and challenging situations.

Another excellent characteristic of the work in this book, which also follows neatly from the selection of behavioral principles at its foundation, is its adherence to objective measurement as a determinant of need and progress. Observing the therapeutic process that families with children in the autism spectrum undergo over the years, we often hear the concern that social skills training can result in few gains even after repeated trials. Some of the disappointment expressed by the parents comes from unrealistic and inflated expectations, in some cases set by the clinicians themselves, as social deficits are indeed at the core of the condition that beset these children. But more often, it is the lack of understanding of where the children's baseline standing in their mastery of the different skills lies at the start of the intervention and the failure to communicate the differential growth that takes place simply because there is no quantification of it. This caveat is avoided in Ms. McKinnon and Ms. Krempa's work with a pre- and post-design that provides both the parent and the professional with much needed quantifiable feedback.

Guided by their clinical orientation at heart, the work produced by Ms. McKinnon and Ms. Krempa is intended to be a blueprint for those professionals working directly with children with social deficits. Its title does justice to the efforts within the work to be a "hands-on manual" for the clinician. Starting with the initial assessment of the child's proficiency prior to the start of the program to the implementation of each of its modules to the smallest details, this book should serve to fulfill the frequently offered recommendation made by diagnosticians that social skills intervention adhere to a well-defined curriculum.

Finally, I could not go without pointing out that, aside from its substantive contributions, the characteristic that makes this manual successful is the unbounded enthusiasm and passion that has driven its creation. In many of the pages, the dedication and care that these two professionals have towards their subjects clearly comes through, making it an outstanding contribution to the overall intervention of children with socialization deficits.

Rafael Castro, Ph.D.
Clinical Neuropsychologist
Licensed Psychologist

Introduction:
Who we are and why we wrote this

This manual is intended for those faced with the challenges of teaching and supporting children with autism every day. As consultants to both school teams and families, we have attempted to keep the language easy to read, however staying true to important principles.

The principles of ABA (Applied Behavioral Analysis) are utilized and explained as they apply to our teaching of social skills. By no means do we provide a comprehensive list of these principles, but we do provide what you'll need to implement our solutions.

The philosophy of the Module System and the Social Skills Checklist is designed for both parents and professionals. It is a starting point to determine appropriate baseline social skills, and a means to develop goals and achieve them. The checklist can be photo-copied, and used with many different children. While parents should be aware that teaching some of these skills will require a group setting, there are many activities that can be worked on in the home or within your family.

The strategies listed under each module are designed to be a starting point and a guide in which to begin your teaching process. The list of worksheets, easy to follow examples of how to use these tools and a comprehensive resource are all provided to successfully implement a social skills program.

As practitioners, we are faced every day with the challenge of developing and teaching appropriate skills for children on the autism spectrum. Teaching social skills has become a popular topic in the world of autism, with many different perspectives of what social skills are and how to teach them. If you ask teachers what social skills are they may include the ability to sit and listen, raise your hand and follow classroom directions. If you ask a speech and language pathologist, they may include the ability to use language or to see someone else's point of view; if you ask a parent, they may say the ability to have friends and spend time with them. Are all of these important social skills? Of course!

In an effort to teach our children effective (opening the door to more opportunities in the future), meaningful (enriching quality of life) and functional (ability to use every day, all day) social skills, we began a literature review of social skills curriculums and texts that were available for teachers and practitioners. We found some very good literature out there about social skills (see Resources). Yet our quest to find an easy to follow and easy to implement social skill assessment tool, encompassing all of the areas we felt were important to the social development of children with autism, was not out there. We wanted a manual that adhered to our clinical beliefs in teaching relevant skills, and generalizing those skills to naturally occurring situations and environments. We wanted a curriculum that was deeply rooted in the idea of positive behavioral support, and we wanted a program that was interesting and fun to implement. We created this one based on our practical experiences.

We hope you find this manual helpful. Some very smart and funny children along the way have taught us very well. It is because of them, and for them, that we write this book.

Do you know a child with autism who...
- Walks the perimeter of the playground at recess instead of playing with peers?
- Eats lunch at a table with an aide or alone, staring off, looking at the wall or at nothing in particular?
- Begins to laugh in class when the teacher is giving a lecture or when the students are assigned small group work to complete a project?
- Has difficulty making conversation at the dinner table?
- Repeats the same questions over and over? Asks the same questions about lawnmowers, or car keys or a certain baseball player?
- Starts to rock or flap his arms when in a small group setting with peers?
- Walks by other students' desks pushing papers and pencils on the floor?
- Hits or pushes peers, even peers that are considered friends?
- Walks over to a group of students playing and knocks down their blocks or runs away with their ball?

We do, too. And that is why we wrote this book.

Our Inspiration:
Success stories from kids we know

One day, while watching a championship basketball game on television, *Noah, who had never sat and watched a game with his dad before, walked in and began telling his dad about the teams. He explained that they were teams because of the different shirts, that each team had their own basket, and that you helped your team-mates. He even went on to say that sometimes he was the captain when he played, and liked being the captain! His father was thrilled! This was one of the first "father-son" moments they had ever had.

Noah's father-son moment is the culmination of learning through the use of video modeling, picture/word-based stories, role-playing, and actual practice playing with both visual supports and a peer buddy. All of these techniques are outlined in this book.

What makes Noah's story all the more remarkable is that he is a third grader diagnosed with mild autism. He participated in a social skills group sponsored by his school district. The group comprised of 3 other students on the spectrum and 4 peer buddies that joined every other session. The main focus was to teach the concepts of social communication through playing games: what it means to be on a team; what it means to have different roles on a team (outfielder vs. kicker); what it means to be a captain; how to play 3 different games with minimal prompting; how to cheer your teammates on; and how to talk about the game afterword with friends.

— Kelly

*Names have been changed to insure confidentiality.

recently went to a birthday party for a child that I had worked with for three years. I had not seen *Andy or his younger brother (whom I had also worked with) in several months, so I was very excited to visit with them.

This birthday party was a swimming party and was going extremely well. One or two peers from Andy's class were enjoying the party too. I gave Andy his birthday present, and he said thank you and opened it. He was, as would be with any eleven year old, more excited about the toy than the t-shirt. He dashed off to return to swimming before we had a chance to chat.

I had also brought a gift for his younger brother, *Jim. I gave it to him, and watched as he opened it. He thanked me flatly for the remote control car and stared at the floor in disappointment.

I tried to explain, "Jim, I hope you like the car. I didn't know what to get you... I haven't seen you in months..."

He quickly replied, "You could have called."

In writing a manual for social skills, I want to be sure to treasure and preserve this kind of honesty, and not just teach conformity and manners. Otherwise, I believe we'd be missing a lot.

— Janis

*Names have been changed to insure confidentiality.

Part 1

• • •

GETTING STARTED

- **Understanding Autism and ABA**

- **Assessment**

- **Building the scaffolding and using the Module System**

- **Strategies to teach skills**

What are social skills?

Social skills are "those behaviors which, within a given situation, predict important social outcomes." In a clinical sense this is true, and as a reference for the rest of the non-scientific community, volumes of books on social skills, manners, and etiquette (including an eight hundred forty-five page book from Peggy Post— of Emily Post heritage) have given us guidelines on how to engage, interact and facilitate social interaction. The books are really about social rules, "What do we do?" "How do we do it?" "When do we do it?" Social skills are the rules and expectations that allow us to connect and be who we are and share who we are. That is why it is so important that we teach these skills to children with autism.

Social rules, explicit and implied, are everywhere. It is easiest, however to notice them when they are missing. When someone stands too close, when someone talks loudly or when someone makes an inappropriate comment.

This has been the case all too often with children with autism. They have been given lots of language and cognitive skills training, however, social skills, the vehicle they need to utilize these learned skills have not been addressed. As a result, these children end up frustrated and socially isolated without a means to communicate and connect with people.

It seems the number of children receiving a diagnosis somewhere on the autism spectrum is on the rise. The causes of autism are still being rigorously researched, and, in the absence of clear causation, we are left with needing to provide treatment.

When looking at autism, it is important to acknowledge that the diagnostic criterion denotes significant impairment in social areas. In addition to language and behavior deficits, the DSM-IV of the American Psychiatric Association (1994) notes these social deficits within the autism diagnosis:

1) Qualitative Social Impairment

a. Marked impairment in the use of multiple nonverbal behaviors such as: eye gaze; facial expression; body postures; and gestures used in social interaction

b. Failure to develop peer relationships appropriate to developmental level.

c. Lack of spontaneity in seeking to share enjoyment, interests, or achievements with other people, as well as, a lack of showing, or pointing to objects of interest.

d. Lack of social or emotional reciprocity

2) Qualitative Impairments in Communication as manifested by at least one of the following:

a. Delay of lack of spoken language

b. In individuals with speech, marked impairment in the ability to initiate or sustain a conversation with others.

c. Stereotyped and repetitive use of language or idiosyncratic language

d. Lack of varied, spontaneous, make believe or social imitative play.

3) Restricted repetitive and stereotyped patterns of behavior, interests and activities

a. Encompassing preoccupation with one or more stereotyped and restricted patterns of interest that is abnormal either in intensity or focus

b. Apparently inflexible adherence to specific, nonfunctional routines or rituals

c. Stereotyped and repetitive motor mannerisms (e.g., hand or finger flapping or twisting, or complex whole body movements)

d. Persistent preoccupation with parts of objects

Comparing the social deficits in the diagnostic criteria, we see that many children with the diagnosis of autism demonstrate a few, some, or all of the skill deficits. How these are manifested in each child is different, but may frequently look like:

Deficits in young children may include:
Few smiles
Poor imitation
Poor eye contact
Poor joint attention
Poor reciprocal play
Little interest in others
Little interest in other children
An increase in aberrant behaviors in new settings or in crowds

Deficits in older children may include:
Difficulty with interests and conversations beyond their interests
Difficulty establishing and/or maintaining friendships
Difficulty understanding non-verbal communication
Difficulty understanding social rules and conventions
Difficulty understanding others feelings
Difficulty with problem solving
Difficulty with flexibility

Before we go any further, we want to comment about this manual. Recognizing that each child with autism may have different learning styles, this is NOT a program book. Instead, we have attempted to provide a detailed skill-based assessment system (the Social Skills Checklist) and a systematic process to develop and build upon these skills (the Module System and Level System presented later in this book). The activities in this book are designed to help you create stimulating and creative activities to address very specific goals and target behaviors for your student(s). In knowing the child, using the assessment, and applying careful task analysis and goal selection procedures, these activities can be further individualized and be very rewarding and motivating for both you and your child.

Teaching relevant and age appropriate social skills needs to be established as a priority in any program, particularly once a form of communication (either verbal or non-verbal) has been developed. This means implementing strategies for basic skills at the beginning of your child's program, and continuing to advocate social skills as a priority in intervention as the child progresses. Many typical ABA programs are rich in academics, which are certainly a priority; we are suggesting that social skills be considered an equal priority in programming.

As academics progress and develop, the child with autism may start to "stand out" socially from other children. He/she with autism may not play with others at recess, may not seek out friends, may not know how to carry on a conversation about the latest movie, or computer game, or join in activities at birthday parties. The social gap between the child with autism and his peers may widen with time, and can become increasingly difficult to repair.

Social success is vital for children at all points on the autism spectrum. We are broadly defining social success as:
1) The ability to get needs met through appropriate and socially acceptable means
2) The ability to share thoughts, feelings and knowledge
3) The ability to participate in social activities with maximum independence

While we believe it is never too late, it is best to start early. We have provided this book as your guide to successfully teaching the skills needed for social success.

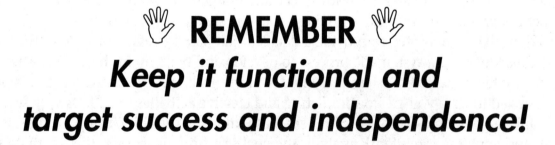

✋ REMEMBER ✋
Keep it functional and target success and independence!

What is ABA and why use this approach to teach social skills?

In 1996 the Early Intervention Program of the New York State Department of Health initiated a comprehensive review of the literature on the different interventions of Autism. The final product, Report of the Recommendations of the Clinical Practice Guidelines: Autism/Pervasive Development Disorders: Evaluation, Assessment, and the Intervention for Young Children, outlines the recommendations of a panel of experts working in the field of autism. The results stated "that the panel strongly recommends implementation of behavioral and educational intervention for children with autism" (and the panel goes on later to say a minimum of 20 hours per week as soon as a diagnosis is made).

> Applied Behavior Analysis (ABA) is a practical approach that uses the principles of learning new skills and technology to change behavior in a systematic and measurable way.

This report also strongly endorses and recommends that the principles of applied behavioral analysis (ABA) be included as a key element of any intervention program for young children with autism to teach language, activities of daily living (self help) and cognitive skills. Using ABA to teach social skills to children with autism is a logical extension of this recommendation.

There are a few principles that we would like to outline that are key points to understand before going on to discuss what and how to teach. As we know, applied behavior analysis is the most well researched and has abundant documentation related to intervention methodologies for teaching children with autism. ABA is both an "instruction book and set of tools". It is NOT a curriculum in and of itself. It is HOW a curriculum is taught to a student, and how that student's progress is measured.

When we refer to ABA in our manual, we are referencing the fundamental principles of ABA, and using them to teach social skills. ABA allows our teaching to be more:

- ○ Systematic- skills are taught in an order that build upon one another; making acquiring the "next step" easier since the prerequisite steps have already been achieved; this is building the scaffolding.
- ○ Accessible and individualized for each child- target skills and behaviors are selected and then broken down into smaller steps so that the child is more likely to be successful
- ○ Discrete- skills are presented with clearly defined expectations so that the child knows exactly what to do to be correct
- ○ Organized-materials, activities and the environment are situated in such a way that maximizes efficiency in the teacher and the child's independence to start, work on and clean up activities with minimal assistance.
- ○ Rewarding- by assessing motivation and interests, and using this information to help teach skills, providing reinforcement on a regular and frequent schedule, the child is more likely to engage in learning.

The "applied" in applied behavior analysis, means functional and meaningful. This means that the child is able to use the skill in context in his/her daily life and in his/her community, where the opportunities to use the skill would be most naturally occurring, and would be reinforced through natural contingencies. For example, learning to put on your shoes to go outside, learning to make a sandwich to get yourself a snack, or learning to gain attention appropriately to engage the people you care about in interaction.

The "behavior analysis" of ABA refers to looking at observable behavior (what you can see) as a means of identifying target skills to work on. Too, "analyzing behaviors," allows us to focus in on target behaviors to determine if they meet the criteria for mastery, or, conversely, to see if we need to continue to work on the skills, and target generalization or fluency (being able to use the skill in "real time" so that it is as natural as possible).

There are several principles that we feel best encompass basic ABA methodology, and we believe these principles are necessary to understand thoroughly before teaching new skills. Here is our 'short version' of the principles and terminology of ABA that relate to teaching methodologies (the "how to") in this manual and for good teaching in general.

1. Baseline information—the skill level at present, before you start teaching. Questions to consider when collecting this information: What skills does the child already have? What can the child do now? With whom can the child do it? Under what conditions is the child successful and unsuccessful? Where? Baseline information is important to define the beginning point, the checklist serves as a baseline survey of skills, from the checklist, take more specific data or notes about certain skills for individual baseline information. Refer to the Social Skills Checklist to assist you in determining baseline information.

2. Functional Analysis—determining, based on data collection, and manipulation of variables, why a particular behavior is happening or not happening by manipulating factors such as precursor events and what happens just following the behavior. A descriptive analysis asks questions about antecedents and following behaviors, and, in addition, where it is occurring (or not occurring), who is present (or not), and even details such as time of day, types of demands, and medical and/or physical conditions that may contribute to the target behavior.

3. Goal selection/prioritizing—determining the appropriate behavior or skill to target can be a challenge. It should be based on baseline information and assessments. Use these questions as guidelines: What is the most difficult part of the day for the child? What makes him stand out most? What is developmentally appropriate? In other words, is there a gap between developmentally appropriate skills and what the child is demonstrating? Use the checklists to help with this. What is the next step in the skill sequence?

4. Task Analysis—the breaking down of a task, behavior or skill into smaller, more manageable components to facilitate learning and, ultimately, success. Focusing on one component or step at a time is a great way to build success and not overwhelm the student with too many or too great expectations.

5. Prompting—there are many prompting strategies to draw from, and indeed there is a prompting hierarchy. When teaching a new skill, we agree it is generally best to provide assistance from the most to the least intrusive. This will insure that the student gets the help he/she needs to secure initial success (a.k.a. "errorless teaching") while minimizing or eliminating mistakes. When prompting a previously acquired or established skill, it is best to use least intrusive prompts to promote maximum independence. (Prompting is also discussed further in the inclusion section of this manual). Keep in mind, that the goal is success and independence. Prompts are listed from most intrusive to least intrusive, but may take many forms:

a. *Full physical prompt* – physical assistance/hand over hand
b. *Tactile prompt* – light touch
c. *Modeling* – demonstrating the skill or behavior to the student
d. *Verbal prompt* – giving the full word or verbal response
e. *Partial verbal prompt* – giving only part of the word, the initial sound of a word or first word in a sentence or a verbal clue to the correct response
f. *Visual prompt and/or textual cues* – a sight word, or picture symbol; many examples are included in this manual
g. *Gestural prompt* – pointing to the correct response
h. *Receptive/expressive latency cues* – waiting for a predetermined length of time before providing assistance
i. *Rehearsal strategies* – practicing the skill or behavior before having to use it

6. The "SD" (discriminative stimulus), is the directive or instruction—its imperative to present very CLEAR expectations to the child so that he/she knows exactly what to do and knows what is considered to be a correct response that will lead to reinforcement.

7. The "reinforcer" or reward is given to the student after a correct response, thereby making it more likely that the correct response will occur again and again in those same circumstances. Remember...the reinforcer must actually be reinforcing to the child (find out what the child likes or prefers), not what we think would be fun to get or get out of (not everyone responds to stickers, sweets or high fives).

8. Progress and measurement—it is important that the team establish and write goals in behavioral terms that can be clearly understood by everyone working with the child and can be definitively measured for progress review. Again, consider these questions when writing goals and target skills: Who will do what, when, under what conditions, with how much support, for how long or how many times, and where?

The most important component of teaching the child with autism is to build towards success by clearly defining the goal, working systematically, consistently and sequentially, and being certain not to overwhelm the child with too many expectations and demands at once.

Most of us are naturally reinforced to be social, meaning that the mere act of talking, playing and sharing is often inherently reinforcing. We know this is often not so for children with autism. It is therefore unlikely that if we 1) wait for a child to emit a natural and appropriate social response, and then 2) reinforce that social response with social praise or another appropriate response, we will probably not encounter many teachable moments or praise worthy opportunities.

Important helpful teaching strategies include:

Rehearsal strategies—practicing the correct responses before the behavior or response is required in the target situation (practicing before entering the classroom what to say when the student sees his friends).

Chaining—
a. Backward chaining: targeting and reinforcing a student for appropriate behavior, skill, or step that occurs at the end of a behavior sequence, then gradually building one step at a time to include the entire sequence. For example, if a student is unable to attend for a 20 minute circle time, begin by having the student enter in the circle with just 3 minutes left until it ends, and she/he can leave the circle successfully and appropriately with peers. Upon successful completion of 3 minutes, gradually add time, introducing the child earlier and earlier into the circle until eventually he is able to begin and end the circle with his peers.
b. Forward chaining: targeting and reinforcing a student for an appropriate behavior, skill, or step that occurs at the beginning of a behavior sequence, gradually building to include the entire sequence. For example, in teaching a student how to get dressed (putting on pants) using forward chaining, one would first reinforce the child for holding the pants the right way and then placing the right foot in the right leg, then the left leg, then pulling the pants up, etc.

Environmental modifications — rearranging the environment or setting to allow target behaviors to occur more easily and/or more naturally. This could mean changing where the child sits, where materials are kept, access to games to take to recess, modification of schedule to minimize transitions, etc.

Modeling — demonstrating exactly what the correct or desired response is. Keep in mind, the teacher, a peer, sibling, or parent can do modeling. It is a prerequisite that the child has imitation skills and understands that he/she should follow/imitate the behavior just observed.

Indirect prompting — this technique is generally best used if a child has previously had an experience with the expected response, and can be used as a prompt-fading process. For example, if you have taught a child to walk over to you when you present markers, and the child is not looking at you, you may knock on the table or make a noise that prompts the child to look at you, and then realize he/she should walk over to initiate interaction.

Building the Scaffolding and Using the Module System

After reviewing much of the current literature, and developing our own strategies and ideas from our practice, we realized that we were looking for a fluid way to teach social skills to children with autism. We've created a path that integrates, in a sequential order, social skills that build on one another, with careful attention not to jump ahead and teach target skills before other relevant pre-requisite skills are mastered. This was important to us, as we often encounter children with "splintered" social capabilities. For example, a child with a "splintered skill" may be able to initiate a conversation with a written script; however that child is not able to respond back to the other person's questions and does not make eye contact— two important skills that are pre-requisites for conversation.

We propose teaching social skills, not as isolated skills, but instead as skill scaffolding, building a progression of skills.

The "scaffolding" or "building" approach to social development is the key to our philosophy. We have broken down the necessary social skills to meet each platform level of the scaffold to be taught in a systematic method. Think of it this way: when you learn to ride a bike you start off on a tricycle, you learn to sit and pedal first, and then to balance. This is also true with teaching social skills; you need to start with a foundation. You can't expect a child to initiate and hold onto topics of conversation if they have yet to learn the skill of responding to basic questions. You can't expect that child to be able to respond to basic questions, until they have learned pre-requisite joint attention skills.

The Module System offers the basic skill sets and scaffolding offers the individualized presentation and progression of these skills.

Base on this theory, we have developed the Module System that looks like this:

Module 1 | **Joint Attention:** Acknowledging and attending to others; maintaining eye contact

Module 2 | **Greetings:** Acknowledging and greeting others, managing your body and personal space

Module 3 | **Social Play:** Interacting with others, in appropriate social contexts, recognizing common interests; engaging in play

Module 4 | **Self Awareness:** Regulating self, delaying reinforcement and self-monitoring appropriately

Module 5 | **Conversation:** Acknowledging and responding to another person's language/conversation thoughtfully, and initiating & sustaining conversations

Module 6 | **Perspective Taking:** Labeling and interpreting personal emotions and other's emotions; showing compassion to another and adapting one's behavior appropriately

Module 7 | **Critical Thinking:** Problem solving, planning and generating options for determining what comes next

Module 8 | **Advanced Language:** Understanding and responding to advanced language: social pragmatics, including interpreting social clues and inferences

Module 9 | **Friendships:** Making & sustaining friendships

Module 10 | **Community Skills:** Independence in the community and in daily life

Our system has been broken down into 3 levels. The levels refer to the depth of each skill in each module. The level of the skill depends on the baseline information for each student. The skill levels are not based on age. Each module contains many skill sets, each at different levels, beginning at its most basic, to the most advanced. In this dynamic process, the student acquires skills and progresses through each level in the module until all 3 levels have been mastered. Please keep in mind that your child may be on Level 2 of Joint Attention skills, but on Level 1 of Greetings.

For example, when teaching Perspective Taking, Module #7 we start off teaching a child to look at and label another person's emotions, Level 1. To move that skill to Level 2 (a more sophisticated level), we teach the child to recognize and respond to the emotion. Finally, we develop this skill even further, to teach the child to modify his/her behavior based on the emotion he/she identified, Level 3, essentially teaching empathy and appropriate emotional responding (a highly sophisticated level). The three distinct levels are building the scaffolding of social communication.

This diagram illustrates the continual process of assessing, learning, and progressing. The Socials Skills Checklist Level System clearly defines each skill within each Module.

Module 1

Level 1 Social Skills Checklist:
This level involves teaching children to begin the process of developing social skills on a basic responding level.
This means learning to attend to situations and acknowledge others, play with toys, and begin to problem solve.

Level 2 Social Skills Checklist:
This level involves teaching children to move beyond basic responding and begin to recognize when to respond and why. It also teaches sustaining responses and moving to higher level skills that may require more then one response, and long-term interactions and responses.

Level 3 Social Skills Checklist:
This level involves teaching children to move beyond sustained responses, to both generalizing skills learned to more natural and meaningful scenarios; to respond to more implicit social rules, self-management, and the ability to demonstrate and understand more refined emotions and perspectives in everyday situations.

Assessments and the Social Skills Checklist

As we've discussed earlier, social skills are the rules and expectations that allow us to connect and be who we are and share who we are. However, there are few comprehensive standardized tests that really address the individual levels of social skills and the precise behaviors that comprise overall "socially skilled" behavior.

Practitioners and psychologists use many different tools to assess social skills. None have expressed to us one tool that seems to offer an accurate and comprehensive picture of current social skill functioning to plan goal selection and interventions. Speech and language pathologists have many assessment tools that they use to help determine social skill needs in the areas of language and social pragmatics and this can be helpful in adding to your own assessments.

Since we have not found one assessment tool that lists all of the skills in all of the areas that we feel are important and crucial for the child with autism, we have created our own Social Skills Checklist.

The Social Skills Checklist has been developed to break down specific social skills within the Module System. There are three separate checklists, representing the three levels of development for each social skill module. These checklists are meant to provide a reference list of skills that are frequently identified as specific areas of need for the child with autism. You will notice that on each of the checklists, across each level, the skills become progressively more sophisticated and detailed.

The list itself is a "work in progress." As social skills, critical thinking and executive functioning become more thoroughly researched, the checklists will undoubtedly be expanded to include these new skills. As we learn what our kids needs are, we will add more. (Feel free to contact us with your suggestions, too!)

It is recommended that the Social Skills Checklist be used to determine pre- and post social skills. The pre-testing will allow for accurate baseline measurement and the post-test will assess for skill acquisition and reliability.

The checklist is also a comprehensive reference tool to facilitate goal planning for IEPs (Individual Education Plans).

The Social Skills Checklist

Name of student _____

Diagnosis _____

Date of pre-test _____

Date of post-test _____

Date of birth _____

Completed by _____

School _____

Teacher _____

Janis Krempa, M.Ed. BCBA
Kelly McKinnon, M.A. BCBA

 # The Social Skills Checklist — Level 1

Student:	Yes/No 1:1	Yes/No In Group	Yes/No Natural Setting
Module 1: Joint Attention/Attending			
Looks when called/comes when called			
Turns and orients toward person when making requests			
Follows eye gaze, point or gesture by others			
Looks/orients/responds to object presented			
Looks/orients when listening to others (shifts body/gaze every few sec.)			
Imitates 1-2 step motor tasks			
Looks expectantly for something to happen			
Sits and attends to simple tasks (10 min)			
Sits quietly in circle			
Imitates hand movements in circle			
Calls out in unison			
Follows basic 1,2 step auditory directions (directed at group)			
Sits next to peers			
Passes item to peers			
Gains appropriate attention of others			
Module 2: Greetings			
Waves			
Says "Hi" in response to greetings			
Walks up to others to greet			
Says "Bye"			
Politeness Marker			
Says "Please"			
Reciprocates affection			
Module 3: Social Play			
Sustains independent play for 15 min. w/close-ended toys i.e. puzzles			
Plays parallel +15 minutes, close to peers w/close-ended toys			
Plays with open ended toys i.e. blocks, trucks, legos (builds)			
Imitates movement with objects			
Imitates peers w/ peer leader in songs, Simon says, etc.			
Imitates up to 4-6 actions in play routines			

The Social Skills Checklist — Level 1

Student: _____	Yes/No 1:1	Yes/No In Group	Yes/No Natural Setting
Module 3: Social Play (continued)			
Takes a turn for 5 turns w/concrete toys i.e. blocks,potato head, swings,etc			
Sustains imaginative play i.e. restaurant, doctor, trucks, etc.for 15min			
w/adult			
w/other child			
Shares toys			
Trades toys			
Stops when peers say "stop"			
Ends play appropriately			
Cleans up toys when done			
Joins in small group free play			
Plays functionally with playground equipment/sustains peer play			
Can sit and play simple game with adults directing			
Module 4: Self Awareness			
Ability to tolerate new demands/tasks with support			
Ability to delay reinforcement up to for 1-2 hours			
Accepts interruptions during preferred activity			
Asks for help vs. task avoidance			
Accepts endings/transitions			
Accepts 1-2 changes in schedule (flexibility)			
Accept changes in play (flexibility with play)			
Module 5: Conversations			
Please work with Speech and Language therapists to be sure that all areas of speech and language are addressed appropriately			
States wants/needs (mands) 30+ per day			
Labels (tacts) up to 100 minimum			
Identifies others by name			
Can answer 1-3 social questions i.e. name, age, family names, pet names			
Answers others appropriately (no echolalia)			
Summons/calls others			
Answers Yes/No questions appropriately			
Asks for information: "What is that?" "Where is it?"			

 # The Social Skills Checklist — Level 1

Student: _____	Yes/No 1:1	Yes/No In Group	Yes/No Natural Setting
Module 5: Conversations *(continued)*			
Intraverbals of: Fill in blank Attributes "What has..."			
Categories "Name some...."			
Answers "Who" questions			
Answers "What" questions			
Describes/comments on own actions i.e. "I am (action)"			
Asks for attention i.e. "Watch me" "Look at me"			
Waits to be called on in a group			
Volunteers information on a topic			
Offers information about school day			
Module 6: Perspective Taking			
Labels/imitates emotions in pictures			
Labels emotions on people, cartoons			
Labels emotions on self			
States what makes child: happy, sad, etc.			
Labels body parts on a person including hair color, eye color, glasses, etc.			
Guesses others imitations of emotions			
Looks for/find hidden objects and hides them			
Plays charades/imitates another character			
Notices & attempts to comfort others			
Module 7: Critical Thinking Skills			
Ability to follow schedule/rules			
Makes choices out of 3			
Understands concept: First, Then			
Can sequence pictures up to 4 steps			
Can retell 4 pictures in sequence			
Can categorize items/themes			
Makes basic inferences- "What do you need?" to finish something or make something			
Retells events in life/visual aide support			
Can find things not present			
Can determine "What is wrong?" (in pictures)			
Can determine "What is same & different?" (in pictures)			
Can name opposites			

©copyright 2005, Social Skills Solutions, reprinted with permission.

 # The Social Skills Checklist — Level 1

Student: _____	Yes/No 1:1	Yes/No In Group	Yes/No Natural Setting
Module 8: Advanced Language			
see level 2			
Module 9: Developing Friendships			
Sits next to same peer consistently			
Plays with same peer(s) across several days and several activities			
Shares (snack/toy) with peer			
Attends birthday party, with peer			
Module 10: Community/Home Life			
Home:			
Voids in toilet			
Undresses when appropriate			
Attempts to dress self			
Tolerates brushing teeth			
Sleeps in own bed			
Sits to eat			
Remains in home safely			
Avoids dangerous situations			
Community: (some examples)			
Stays with parents in community (up to 20 min)			
Go to doctor's appt. successfully			
Stays with family in shopping malls/stores			
Plays near/with peers in community (bikes, ball, trucks, dolls, etc.)			
Holidays:			
Birthday-follows schedule			
Waits while others open presents			
Halloween- tolerates costume			
Walks w/family			
Other holidays:			
Sits w/family at meals			
Other areas of need:			

 # The Social Skills Checklist — Level 2

Student: _____	Yes/No 1:1	Yes/No In Group	Yes/No Natural Setting
Module 1: Joint Attention/Attending			
Orients toward person when speaking/listening			
Listens quietly when appropriate			
Repeats back directions 2-3 steps and completes action			
Can sit and listen to group stories			
Shows others objects w/intent to share			
Points to objects to share			
Follows other's eye gaze to objects			
Follows basic non-verbal commands ex: stop, open arms, finger shake-no, point-look			
Knows place and stays in line			
Walks in pace with others			
Can look and judge if ok to start by others body language/eye gaze-social reference			
Follows instructions to get items/supplies			
Module 2: Greetings			
Greets/waves "Hi" with person's name			
Holds eye contact 1-3 sec. during greeting			
Waves/says "bye" with person's name			
Politeness Marker			
Uses "Thank you" appropriately			
Uses "Sorry" appropriately			
Asks for affection (hug, etc)			
Provides help to others when asked			
Module 3: Social Play			
Can engage in non-physical play			
Can play on own up to 30 minutes			
Can follow playground rules			
Asks 1-3 peers to play their choice			
Can joint play/build/work on simple project together			
Asks 1-3 peers to join in their play			
Sustains play up to 20 min. with peers			
Let's another child choose toy first			
Tolerates other's choice in play			
delaying own choice for another time			

©copyright 2005, Social Skills Solutions, reprinted with permission.

 # The Social Skills Checklist — Level 2

Student: _____	Yes/No 1:1	Yes/No In Group	Yes/No Natural Setting
Module 3: Social Play (continued)			
Can play 2-3 ball/outdoor games for + 20 min. with group +5 peers			
Accepts being called "out"			
Accepts losing games			
Wins gracefully			
Uses free time appropriately			
Plays and sustains board games			
Shifts play ideas w/others, and sustains			
Follows play/understands game/who's "it"			
Imitates actions/speed of actions			
Follows auditory directions-time, sequence directionality (first, middle, 2nd from last)			
Module 4: Ability to Calm Self			
Ability to tolerate new tasks willingly			
Ability to play games & stick with game to the end			
Ability to delay reinforcement: several hours (until Lunch/Dismissal)			
Follows general classroom rules			
Raises hand and waits to talk			
Shares materials with others calmly			
Recognizes and asks for breaks and access to items to calm oneself			
Accepts "No" for an answer			
Expresses anger appropriately			
Accepts when things are different then planned			
Accepts feedback/being corrected/being wrong			
Ability to protest/tell others to "stop"			
Recognizes own space/doesn't touch others			
Module 5: Conversations			
Uses appropriate voice level/tone			
Gains appropriate attention			
Answers +5 questions of own interest			
Answers questions of non-interest (w/adult/peers)			
Has working knowledge/use of pronouns			
Describes using pronouns			
Asks for things using pronouns			
Has working knowledge of adjectives/adverbs			

 # The Social Skills Checklist — Level 2

Student: _____	Yes/No 1:1	Yes/No In Group	Yes/No Natural Setting
Module 5: Conversations *(continued)*			
Comments on actions in games ex: " I have that ___ " " I am doing ___ "			
Can state likes/common interests ex: child responds to peer:"I like that movie too!"			
Can compare own items with others ex:"I don't have that, I have this" (for lunch)			
Talks about immediate past/future			
Talks about current events/movies			
Tells +3 simple jokes			
Answers more complex Intraverbals:			
Abstract categories ex: Name "things that make noise"			
Time of events ex: "When do you eat breakfast?"			
Labels by feature, name ex: "Name some big animals."			
Answers "Where" questions			
Answers "Why" questions			
Comments on others actions/activities ex: "I like your picture"			
Module 6: Perspective Taking			
Describes physical features (including: hair color, glasses, facial hair) (to increase ability to attend to pertinent info)			
Respects personal space of family, friends and strangers			
In pictures, determines cause for emotion			
In people, determines cause for emotion			
In movies, looks at social cues for emotions			
Can look at pictures and understand shared/not shared experiences			
States self affirmations/emotion ex: "I am good at that" or "I'm sad"			
States "likes" about others ex: "I like your shirt"			
Can observe social cues in pictures			
Understands roles of various community helpers			
Module 7: Problem Solving			
Critical Thinking Skills			

The Social Skills Checklist — Level 2

Student:	Yes/No 1:1	Yes/No In Group	Yes/No Natural Setting
Module 7: Problem Solving (continued)			
Can generate "what comes next"			
Retells events of that day/yesterday			
Retells short stories w/out visuals			
Can do word associations - oral categories (with quick response time)			
Can identify what is missing in pictures, objects, etc.			
Short-term memory:			
recalls 3-5 pictures shown			
recalls 3-5 items shown			
repeats 3-5 verbal directions			
Ablity to use self-talk as a rehearsal strategy			
Ability to use self talk as a reminder of what to do			
Separates 3-4 parts of simple story: characters/action/location			
Can generate (verbal) list of items needed ex: for lunch, or music			
Describes basic themes "at night, we do this"			
Understands concept of safe vs. dangerous			
Can choose which item does not belong			
Can give basic reasons "why" in pictures/events			
Writes a story (subject/title, characters, setting)			
Module 8: Advanced Language			
Language pragmatics *refer to speech and language assessments			
Understands 10-15 common idioms			
Understands concept of lies vs. truths			
Talks about plans for the future			
Can compare items and explain same/different			
Explains the main idea of a simple story			
Is beginning to read			
Module 9: Friendships			
Gives others compliments			
Says "thank you" to compliments			
Answers truthfully about things (including wrong-doings)			

 # The Social Skills Checklist — Level 2

Student: _____	Yes/No 1:1	Yes/No In Group	Yes/No Natural Setting
Module 9: Friendships (continued)			
Provides apology to others when appropriate			
Helps others when asked			
Invites friends over for play dates			
Engages in scheduled play with play date			
Walks w/ a group of friends			
Acknowledges others as friends & why			
Module 10: Community/Home			
Home:			
Knows address/phone number			
Knows family members' names			
Knows birthday			
Clears plate/cup when done			
Cleans up spills			
Answers telephone and gets appropriate person			
Gets along with siblings			
Community:			
Stays with family in community & participates			
Can make basic purchases			
Has appropraite restaurant behavior			
Waits with family at cross-walk			
Holidays:			
Accepts undesirable gifts graciously ex: says "thank you" vs. "I didn't want this"			
Knows and can explain individual holidays			
Follows basic family traditions			
Other areas of need:			

 # The Social Skills Checklist — Level 3

Student:	Yes/No 1:1	Yes/No In Group	Yes/No Natural Setting
Module 1: Joint Attention/Attending			
Can repeat and perform 4-5 step directions			
Can listen and take notes			
Follows and completes large group instruction (whole class)			
Can follow test-taking instructions			
Notices and gets the attention of others when necessary			
Uses gestures to communicate			
Module 2: Greetings			
3-part greeting ex: "Hi, How are you, name?"			
2-3 part inquiries ex: "Where is...your brother?"			
Politeness Markers			
Acknowledges bumping into others			
Asks family/ friend about day			
Resonds "You're welcome" appropriately			
Corrects others nicely or politely overlooks mistakes			
Shows concern and asks "Are you OK?" ex: peer is coughing			
Receives compliments well			
Module 3: Social Play			
Sustains play of choice with group + 30 min			
Sustains play of other's choice +20 min			
Sustains play: ball games +30 min			
Sustains play: other games ex: tag, chase, etc			
Will join in recess play willingly			
Deals with teasing appropriately			
Stays with a team-follows team in game/cheering/rules			
Accepts ideas/changes in game			
Cheers other on			
Awareness of pop culture games/play			
Module 4: Ability to Calm Self			
Ability to work towards reinforcement for 1-2 days			
Accepts authority from adults/peers			
Decreases target behaviors 0-2 severe per week			

 # The Social Skills Checklist — Level 3

Student: _____	Yes/No 1:1	Yes/No In Group	Yes/No Natural Setting
Module 4: Ability to Calm Self (continued)			
Accepts making mistakes/accepts other's mistakes			
Handles constructive criticism/attempts change			
Refuses requests of other's appropriately			
Questions what might be unjust			
Responds appropriately to bullying			
Responds to teasing appropriately			
Responds to physical assault appropriately			
Self-regulates arousal level			
Module 5: Conversations			
Remains quiet when others talk			
Paces self-waits for pauses to answer/start questions			
Interrupts appropriately ex: raises hand in class ex: waits for break in conversation with friends			
Maintains conversation for 6 exchanges by answering questions and asking questions to gather information			
Identifies topic & comments on topic			
Initiates topics and holds conversation			
Discusses common interests ex: "I like that too- do you?"			
Requests information from others ex: "Where did you get that?" ex: "What do you do with that?"			
Tells +5 jokes to peer/group			
Can shift topics up to 3 topics			
Watches for listener confirmation before continuing conversation			
Ends conversation appropriately			
Module 6: Perspective Taking			
Recognizes/interprets body language			
Recognizes other's more complex emotions			
Stops behavior based in response to other's emotions: ex: sad, bored, frustrated, etc			
Can explain own emotions			
Recognizes when others do something nice			
Identifies nice vs. mean vs. teasing			

# The Social Skills Checklist — Level 3

Student:	Yes/No 1:1	Yes/No In Group	Yes/No Natural Setting
Module 6: Perspective Taking (continued)			
Shows empathy toward others			
Follows more complex social rules ex: "majority rules"			
Detects level of interest from other's in activity			
Uses appropriate language to express dislike			
Accepts other's likes and tolerates them			
Concerned about what others think, what their "reputation" is			
Module 7: Problem Solving			
Asks for clarification			
Recalls/discusses past events +3			
Makes predictions ex: "What will happen & why"			
Interprets idioms			
Understands inferences, paraphrases			
Paraphrase/summarizes			
Knows facts from opinions			
Decodes content of story			
Writes a story (subject/title, characters, setting, main idea/action, details)			
Relays pertinent information			
Keeps calendar to organize self			
Can explain cause & effect & how to change			
Makes deductions from short stories			
Module 8: Advanced Language			
*Refer to speech and language assessment			
Ablilty to interpret gestures/body language			
Ablilty to understand the main idea of a story			
Ablilty to recite/write a personal narrative			
Ablilty to recite/write a descriptive narrative			
Ablilty to recite/write a procedural narrative			
Identifies and understands homonyms			
Identifies and understands synonyms			
Identifies and understands antonyms			
Module 9: Friendships			
Defends self/others verbally/appropriately.			

The Social Skills Checklist — Level 3

Student:	Yes/No 1:1	Yes/No In Group	Yes/No Natural Setting
Module 9: Friendships (continued)			
Introduces self to others			
Lends possessions when asked			
Asks permission to use other's possessions			
Expresses enthusiasm over others comments/ possessions/job well done			
Invites friends over			
Responds to invitations			
Beginning sexuality-address as needed and appropriate ex: knows what is private			
Module 10: Community/Home			
Home:			
Dresses age/peer appropriate			
Follows basic 3-4 step bedroom cleaning routine			
Completes other household chores, ex: feed pet, clean dishes, take out trash, etc.			
Can make him/herself lunch			
Can prepare 1-3 meals			
Orders in restaurant appropriately			
Knows and executes home routine for fire safety			
Knows how to use the stove safely			
Can get help in an emergency			
Recognizes need for 911			
Knows what to do if there's a stranger at the door			
Calls someone on the phone, carries on a 4+ exchange conversation			
Community:			
Utilizes crosswalks and looks both ways			
Joins friends in community events			
Doesn't talk to strangers			
Remains safe in community events			
Knows how to get help			
Other areas of need:			

Teaching Strategies

After using the Social Skills Checklist to determine what specific skill areas your child needs to improve on, we look to the module system. The module system outlines recommended instructional strategies to begin teaching necessary skills. As your child progresses through each module, the skills will build upon previously mastered goals. This allows your child to generalize skills and keeps failure and frustration to a minimum.

Module 1: Joint Attention

The goal of Module 1 is teach your child the ability to acknowledge others in our world and to attend to relevant stimuli. The importance of teaching eye contact and joint attending skills to children with ASD has been established as important pre-requisites for language and play skills. Children with ASD have deficits in responding correctly to the point/gesture of others, or initiating communication with gestures with the purpose of sharing. Additionally, children with ASD have difficulty determining the most meaningful feature of a given stimulus (Frith & Baron-Cohen, 1987). These children focus on fewer features or less relevant cues. As the number of cues in natural contexts increases, responses to those cues decreases (Pierce, Glad, & Shreibman, 1997) as the child must continuously work to determine the most salient stimulus.

There is also evidence that children with ASD have difficulty not necessarily in acquiring and discriminating novel stimuli, but in learning the meaning that is attached to those stimuli. The challenge arises when the child must learn what the symbol means, and learn how to use it and how to integrate and relate it to other information already learned. Much as you are doing right now as you read and digest this information, so it is for your child. Think now of all the nonverbal communication signals, gestures, facial expressions, voice and volume, common community signs, etc, that are stimuli your child needs to interpret.

What does all this mean? This difficulty in joint attention or awareness of others in increasing detail results in:
   o A child that is not able to follow a point cue to share a common point of reference at a distance

○ A child that never seems to "come out of their own world"

○ A child that talks, but never in the direction of anyone

○ A child that only interacts with others when blurting out their favorite things in no specific direction

○ A child that has limited attention and participation in group activities

Because of these fundamental difficulties in joint attention and determining and attending to important stimuli, children with ASD struggle, particularly in a group situation. Looking at our practical teaching, we can address this topic in several ways:

○ Develop instructional control enabling you to then teach a pattern of reliable responding

○ Teach your child to "Look" for a reason (teaching program to follow!)

○ Develop attending and sustained attention skills

○ Teach your child to systematically attend to relevant cues

*See other social skill areas in this book that break this down even further.

Developing attending and instructional control

Developing good attending skills and a pattern of responding is often the first step when working with a child with ASD. This involves the systematic pairing of yourself with reinforcement and then generating a stimulus transfer. If you are reinforcing to be around, a pattern is developed. Now, slowly build in demands-pairing continuous reinforcement for each demand. Again, you develop a pattern of responding. Now, slowly decrease your reinforcement. We cannot say enough about this. It does not mean forcing a child to sit—it means making your teaching fun so they are motivated to sit and attend.

"Look, for a reason"

Not being satisfied with typical "eye contact" strategies found in many traditional ABA/discrete trial programs, we have further detailed this skill from our practical experience with students. We want to teach children to look socially, for a reason. We also want to make eye contact functional for children. The reason why *we* look at one another is to gain more information, to reference one another, and to anticipate.

Continually prompting children to "look at me" was not effective. Instead we created some strategies to teach "looking" that were naturally reinforcing, then shaped the "looking" behavior and rapidly generalized it to more natural settings.

You will notice that not a lot of language is used in this first module. The idea is to teach a child to look, attend to social cues, and reference others. There is no need to confuse the child with too many cues and too much language here.

| Module 1 | Strategies for Teaching Joint Attention |

- Use the Social Skill Checklist to determine your child's baseline level and goals.
- Hold a preferred item to your face and when eye gaze to the item occurs, give the item to the child. Next step: Change this by holding up a preferred item off to one side, point to it, then bring it back to your face-as eye gaze tracks preferred item, give the item to the child. Continue to mastery.
- Do something fun and physical with the child, like giving airplane rides. Once the child experiences what you are doing, pause and wait, as soon as the child looks to you in anticipation-provide the fun airplane ride. Slowly increase the time between the look and the delivery!
- Play fun peek-a-boo and hide and chase games, using the above procedure to teach the "look, for a reason", eye gaze to you starts the game.
- Practice "eye tracking": Hold a favorite object, have the child watch it as you move it back and forth. Move this object in front of your face, and move with the object. As the child masters this, use smaller and smaller objects, eventually moving to a sticker on your face. The child should focus on the sticker as you move.
- Place stickers on your face, have the child search and scan for stickers-next you can add language- "I see it".
- Play Red Light/Green Light with red and green signs. The child has to start and stop to this visual cue. As the child masters this, have a peer lead the game and then move on to head gestures for go (yes) and stop (no).
- Teach a child to determine "Yes" or "No". For example, give the child a task such as where to place a puzzle piece based on your head nodding or shaking in reference to the desired location.
- In a group, have one child put a sticker on his/herself and have your child enter the room, search and scan to see who has the sticker. Have the child say "you have it" and have the other children reward back socially, first with tangible reinforcers (like a sticker or treat), and then shape to more social reinforcement such as hi-fives.
- Put objects on a table, start with 2 objects and slowly increase the number of objects based on your child's success. The child must determine what you are looking at or what you want by following your eyes. Do the same looking around the room. Switch and have your child look at an object for you to figure out what your child is focusing on.

Module 1	Strategies for Teaching Joint Attention *(continued)*

- Play interactive games. This teaches your child to begin to play in a group and attend to the main feature/event. You may need to prompt these initially, and then fade your prompts. Try games, such as "hot potato" sitting in a circle (child must pass something to the person sitting next to them). This is fun with water balloons, where you have to gently pass it to the child next to you and make sure they have it before you let go.

- Play other games such as giving a hi-five and passing it on or "telephone" (where one child starts by whispering a word or short phrase to the child next to him/her and the phrase gets past around until the last person says it out loud). Play pat-a-cake games or Miss Mary Mack hand games. These games will all probably need prompting at first, but with the right prompt-fading procedure, the child will begin to interact with other children.

- Sitting close, roll a ball back and forth with your child, using a roll truck, car or funny toy. Now stand up and expand the distance, and then add in more people.

- Imitate clapping patterns or bouncing ball patterns. Start with simple 1 step imitations and then gradually become more advanced.

- Set up an obstacle course and have children follow each other. Slowly take away the course, and shape it to play follow the leader. Take turns with who is the leader. To advance it, use music and play musical chairs. Prompt for success and quickly fade.

More Advanced:

- In a group, make your own "Guess Who" game. Write up cards that describe facial features about other children in the group or give a verbal description if reading is an issue, systematically decrease the number of features and have your child search and scan to identify the correct person. When your child guesses correctly, have the other child reinforce the social exchange first with tangibles, and then socially with hi-fives.

- Have the child talk with a peer about their favorite topics, facing each other. (If you need to, intermittently reinforce this exchange with tangibles).

- Be sure your child is looking AND listening. Have your child listen to what you are saying, and then have him/her repeat it back to another person. Make errors intentionally, such as talking with your back facing the children, or whispering and have your child notice and correct the errors, then have them watch for their own!

Module 2: Greetings

Why is greeting others so important? It is often the first encounter we have with another person. It's how we make friends and how we introduce ourselves to others. It is this first initial "snap shot" or impression of another person upon which we or they may base subsequent interactions. If someone doesn't acknowledge your child, he/she may feel slighted. Conversely, if a child with ASD does not acknowledge or greet his/her peers, the peers may feel slighted and change their opinion of that child. For many parents, the first time a child does not respond to a greeting from a grandparent or neighbor can be very uncomfortable. It's important for parents to recognize whether or not this is the beginning stage of "avoiding" social situations.

For our children, greetings should be brief; yet they are a good way to build successful social interactions at school and in the community.

Module 2 | Strategies for Teaching Greetings

- Use the Social Skills Checklist to determine your child's baseline level and goals.
- Teach children to simply respond to greetings by others. Teaching the child to respond "Hi" to your saying "Hi" first. Practice this many times, until the skill is mastered. Do not simply wait for greeting opportunities; they occur too infrequently for mastery.
- If saying "Hi" does not prompt your child to respond correctly, try using a visual. Write the word "Hi" on a card and hold it in the palm of your hand, enter a room and wave "Hi" with the visual in your hand, and teach the child to respond "Hi" to that visual. Next, fade the visual until the child responds "Hi" to the hand wave (without the card) and verbal prompt of "Hi". Generalize this to other people and other locations. Slowly fade your wave, to just entering the room and saying "Hi", without the wave. Note on reinforcement: reciprocating the greeting is probably not reinforcing enough for your child initially. Choose reinforcement carefully and fade quickly to socially appropriate responses.
- Teach your child to initiate and greet like other children: use video modeling and visual cards to practice in 1:1 situations "Hi, what's up?" or "Hey". (Do a little investigating and research what the other kids are saying. You want the response to be as natural sounding as possible).

Module 2	Strategies for Teaching Greetings *(continued)*

- ○ Expand your greeting to more natural situations. For example, practice greeting teachers and the principal or other school staff each day, and pick a couple (or all children in his/her classroom) to have the child greet each day. Practice greeting children in the neighborhood. Use the process above, to try and develop an independent (not prompted) greeting, as well as initiated/spontaneous greeting.
- ○ Build greeting opportunities into your day. Your child should use greetings when entering a classroom, going out for recess (*see recess scheduling), joining others for gym or music, going to speech or OT/PT or passing someone in the hall. Making it part of a schedule will help with consistency so it doesn't feel so random for the child and unclear when to demonstrate.

More Advanced:

- ○ Teach non-verbal cues that accompany greetings (waves, hi-5, head nod, smile, etc.).
- ○ Teach the "Hi Smile". The social smile that acknowledges someone, but doesn't actually require a conversation or exchange of words. Start with modeling and imitation, if necessary move to verbal prompting, but fade quickly.
- ○ Teach greetings that are appropriate for different people; family, friends, teachers, clergy, store clerks, etc. Spend some time at this point with some stranger training: whom it is ok to greet, and who it is not. You may need to set clear criteria for this. For example, if you've seen them before you say "Hi", if you haven't ever seen them before (therefore a stranger), do not. If it's someone working in a store or restaurant, etc. then it's ok to greet that person. Use social stories and role-play to teach the social rules and nuances to greetings, because it can be confusing. When it's appropriate for your child, you may need to "set up" natural occurring situations in the community to further facilitate learning. It's important for the community worker to respond to your child for reinforcement.
- ○ Teach greetings that are appropriate for different occasions, holidays, (ex. Happy Birthday, Happy Holidays!, Trick or Treat), at a friend's house, at a store, etc.
- ○ Practice responding to "openers" from other people. Start by teaching your child to respond to, "What did you do today"? Use visuals to help the child graphically organize their day, and then use this to respond appropriately. See appendix for visual tools to use. Then your child can move on to answering more abstract questions like "What's up?" or "How's it going?" or "How was your day?"
- ○ Teach conversation openers, such as "What's up" or "What are you doing". Start with a video of different openers, and then practice with visual cues. Help the child determine conversation openers that they would like to use.

Module 2	Strategies for Teaching Greetings *(continued)*

○ Sample greeting/conversation opener script (use pictures or words as appropriate)
Your child: "Hey dude, whatcha doing?"
Waits for answer
Your child: "Can I play too?"

Introduction
    Your child: "Hi, my name is _____. "
    "What's your name?"

Teach closure: "Bye" or "See you later" or "I gotta go home now"

Module 3: Social Play

Module 3 addresses the ability to interact with another person, through appropriate social contexts and common interests, specifically through play.

A lack of "functional play" is often a significant characteristic of children with ASD. Remember, the diagnostic criteria for autism is narrow, inflexible interests and/or non-interest in others and objects, an exclusive pre-occupation with one or more stereotypical behaviors, and restricted patterns of interest that are either atypical in intensity or focus.

Typically, play for a child with ASD manifests in: a desire to be removed from the play group or uncooperative in a play group setting; fixation on a specific toy or toys including but not limited to spinning wheels on a car or repeatedly opening and closing cabinet doors; or fixation on an activity like walking and following lines on rugs or following along the wall; a rigid pattern of play and lack of flexibility; and behaviors linked with visual tracking. Keep these characteristics in mind when trying to create appropriate play goals for your child. The goal is to teach your child play that includes creative, flexible, purposeful and imaginative interactions independently and with a partner or a group.

We believe play is one of the beginning steps in social development for children, and therefore, it is fundamentally important in early intervention and teaching. See appendix for play skills teaching resources.

In his book Asperger's Syndrome, Tony Attwood describes the importance of play development and notes that during the preschool years, children gradually change from playing alongside someone to playing with someone, and the definition of a friend becomes based on proximity—who they're playing with. He goes on to describe further developmental milestones (taken from research by Roffey, Tarrant and Majors, 1994), and comments that children then start to understand that there is an element of reciprocity needed to maintain friendships, as children learn to share and work together, complimenting and commenting along the way. This reinforces our belief that play is a necessary element of the development of friendships and must be taught to children with ASD.

When we look at play as a series of behaviors and skills, there are many levels and steps building the complexity of play. Here is our developmental play breakdown, based on our readings and observations:

- *Supported play* with closed-ended toys (toys with distinct beginning and endings like puzzles)
- *Independent play* with closed-ended toys
- Beginning *parallel play* (alongside peers)with closed-ended toys
- *Imitation* of movements with an adult (ex. Simon Says)
- *Imitation* of movements to songs (first 1:1, and then in increasingly larger groups ex. Hokey Pokey)
- *Functional play*, beginning of imaginative play
- *Functional imaginative play*, parallel
- Begin *sharing* toys
- Begin *turn-taking* with favorite toys
- *Sitting for a story* (first 1:1, and then in increasingly larger groups)
- *Follows rules* of playground/games appropriately
- *Recess play*:
  - Functional use of equipment for sustained time
    - Expand to include parallel play
    - Expand to include dramatic/symbolic play games (monsters, good/bad guy)
    - Expand to begin ball sports, including concepts of teams, turn taking, and rules as explained further below
- *Advanced imitation* – follow the leader, charades, etc.
- Ability to play board/card games, 1:1 and then in increasingly larger groups
- *Initiates play*
- *Engages in non-preferred play* to stay with group (friends)
- *Accepts losing* or being "called out"
- Sustains *group play* for up to 30 minutes
- Ability to *shift play* as rules change subtly

You will find all of these skill areas in the appropriate level of the Social Skills Checklist as part of the skill assessment process.

It may be necessary to teach these play skills to the child in a 1:1 setting initially. Once you have done so, however, it is extremely important to generalize these skills. In other words, make sure the child is able to perform the skills with other children, in other environments and with other materials. This often requires a great deal of work, and systematic planning and reinforcement for the child.

So, here are a few *general teaching suggestions*:
- Use reinforcing and interesting materials when teaching play.
- Use toys with obvious purposes and then generalize materials and toys to address flexibility, giving your child a lot of toys to choose from.
- Increase access to these toys when the child is not in teaching sessions to encourage generalization opportunities.
- Be sure to teach other people in the child's environment (siblings, para-professionals, etc.) how to play with the toys so they can prompt and encourage play with the same materials, again building generalization.

As children grow older "play skills" may be expanded to include "recreation and leisure skills" and they will need to learn how to effectively and appropriately structure free time, alone and with friends. Leisure skills may include:
- Reading a book or completing a puzzle
- Shopping (appropriate shopping mall behavior and/or grocery shopping)
- Playing miniature golf
- Going to the movies with friends
- Watching a video, alone or with friends
- Eating out with friends or at a friend's home
- Developing art or musical skills
- Playing video games, alone and with friends
- Participating in school activities (dances, sporting games, social functions)
- Trying out for and joining sports teams

Module 3 — Strategies for Teaching Play

- Use the Social Skill Checklist to determine your child's baseline level and goals.

Since you are teaching new skills, remember to use frequent reinforcement and activities of interest whenever possible. Start slow building skill sets with task analysis (systematic breakdown of skills) and use shaping techniques described earlier.

| Module 3 | Strategies for Teaching Play *(continued)* |

○ Teach your child to play with many different closed-ended toys: Once he/she can play with several toys, begin to chain this play together to increase the duration of play. Use a visual schedule or system to do this. Set the toys out, and have your child play with each toy, following a picture schedule. At the end of the picture schedule (and play sequence), teach your child to clean up, and find a parent to earn reinforcement. This can be taught by using a prompt-fading process to independence.

○ Teach imaginative play by a similar process. Set up an imaginary play sequence, such as using a doctor kit. Use video modeling or a visual script to demonstrate a child playing with the kit. Then, teach the child the play sequence as in the model. Use this to teach other imaginative play sequences. Caution: your child's play should be relevant and appropriate, but doesn't have to be exact or too scripted. The goal is for play to be natural and spontaneous.

○ Expand your independent activity schedule to include both closed-ended toys as well as imaginative play toys.

○ In the classroom, or at home, set up play stations using picture schedules to sequence the different stations, similar to the methods above.

○ Systematically monitor generalization of skills in a group. Some children need lots of time working with first 1 other child, then 2 children, then a small group, before they can "jump in" to a group play situation, other children can move quickly to a group after a skill is mastered, don't move too fast.

○ Teach your child to "pick a friend and join in". Do this at first through rehearsal and reinforcement of joining into a known play task with a peer model. Fade your prompts, and then simply schedule it into the day. Reinforce!

○ Note the importance of imitation in play. Children learn typically from watching and practicing what they see others doing. Systematically teach and practice imitation, first with simple motor movements and song imitations, and then to more complex games such as Simon Says and Charades. When prompting your child, it can be helpful to prompt by pointing to what a peer is doing. Reinforce this good imitation.

○ Video modeling with peers is an invaluable tool for teaching play. Video peers playing appropriately and have the child watch and then re-enact the play scene.

○ Help with recess by setting up a schedule- either with pictures or written. We know many children with ASD do well with this type of scheduling, and recess can be otherwise overwhelming. Start with simple steps, such as playing with equipment: "slide, climb, slide, swing". Then build initiation of greetings into your schedule, and then joining in other's play: sample schedule:

| Module 3 | Strategies for Teaching Play *(continued)* |

1) Climb on Toy
2) Slide
3) Go to other slide
4) Say "Hi" to a friend
5) Ask friend to swing
(or join in a game of handball)*see appendix for visual sample.

○ Expand this to using a friend chart. Set up a recess schedule with pictures of class mates and "buddies" and have your child find a friend and join in their play, or ask to play with them. See appendix for a visual example.

○ Teach your child to play ball games and other games. This may mean breaking down each step and practicing (task analysis). A good way to do this is with video modeling, visual story, and then a task analysis of each step. For example, to teach kickball show a video and a visual story. Have the children wear different colored shirts and practice determining who is on what team by having children line up and group together; "all orange shirts stand by the tree, all black shirts stand by the cone". Teach how to kick and run. Teach what bases are and how to run them. Teach what the outfield means. The list goes on and on, but teaching these basic concepts and reinforcing both with tangibles and socially as you go will go a long way in the social development of your child! Video taping the game and showing who and where people are and what their "job" is can also be helpful (this works for teaching how to play tag, too!). Remember to further break down any steps that your child is having trouble with.

○ Set up a home play date, first with one friend, then two. Then go to a friend's house. Setting up an activity schedule, with the skills noted above will help all of the children involved. It could include: 1) saying "Hi", 2) going into a room to play, 3) playing your friend's choice, 4) your choice, 5) having a snack, 6) computer game turn taking! Keep it short and simple at first.

○ Lunch is not the time for paraprofessionals to socialize and take breaks. This is the most important part of the day for the child with ASD. This is when support is needed MOST. All of the diagnostic criteria are center stage in these environments; therefore, ensure that your child is fully supported in these environments. Develop this schedule and philosophy with your school.

Module 4: Self-Awareness

Module 4 will help you teach your child to calm him/herself, self monitor and interact in the world. Frequently children with ASD are seen engaging in repetitive (opening and closing a book), stereotypical (rocking or self-talk behaviors), self-stimulatory (picking at fingers, humming) or maladaptive behaviors (screaming, running in circles or shrieking). These behaviors can occur for any number of reasons, including some legitimate sensory issues. However, more often these behaviors occur because the child is overwhelmed with social, language and behavioral demands. The desire or the demand to participate in an activity without possessing the proper skills can be overwhelming, and/or over stimulating for a child, of any age.

We have found that children are often engaging in these behaviors because: (1) they do not know how else to cope or (2) they do not have generalized skills to handle the situation. Either is reason enough to include coping strategies and anxiety management in a social skills curriculum.

The first step in intervention is helping the parent/teacher/child to recognize when and why these maladaptive behaviors are occurring. Data should be collected for baseline measurement to determine the priority behaviors to tackle. Conducting a functional behavior assessment will help to determine both why a behavior is occurring and what is maintaining that behavior, and from there you can more readily determine an appropriate alternative or replacement behavior. Keep in mind, that for the child to "switch" to more socially appropriate behaviors, the "new" behavior has to effectively meet the needs that the old behavior met whenever possible and sometimes, may need to be incompatible with the "old" behavior.

We will highlight a few interventions that have been successful in our practice when teaching appropriate replacement behaviors. For severe and safety related behaviors, it is recommended that a full functional assessment be completed before an intervention is created to insure maximum replacement skill efficacy.

Generally, after the behavior to be targeted has been identified and brought to the child's attention, a new more appropriate skill/behavior replacement is introduced and practiced, with increased levels (frequency and intensity) of reinforcement for practicing and using the new skill. A plan to decrease the old behavior may also be needed. Consult with your behavior analyst for best practice techniques.

| Module 4 | Strategies for Teaching Self Awareness |

○ Use the Social Skill Checklist to determine your child's baseline level and goals.

Before you make any treatment determinations, you need to look at the function of a behavior- and determine what is maintaining that behavior, what is the child "getting out of" that behavior, what keeps it going? Once you know that, you need to stop allowing that behavior to be reinforced, don't allow your child to get what they need from that behavior. Instead, try these other techniques:

1) Teach a new, more appropriate skill, errorlessly. When teaching a new skill to replace the behavior you are trying to decrease, prompt the child as necessary to perform the correct response (do not allow an error) and then systematically fade your prompting to ensure success. This will prevent the child from making errors, which requires correction, and can result in frustration. Reinforce this new skill, access to what the child was trying to obtain from the maladaptive behavior is the best means to truly reinforce this new skill if it is not disruptive to your child or others around him/her.

2) Differential reinforcement. There are many ways to do this, but a quick suggestion is to reinforce the child for behaviors that occur the correct/desired way, and to not allow reinforcement for the other inappropriate behaviors. Another way to do this is to only provide reinforcement if the target behavior is absent. (If your child calls out, reinforce frequently for the time that they are quiet). Spend time arranging situations for the child to engage in behaviors that will help this, and be ready with reinforcement.

3) Time-out from positive reinforcement. Be very careful with time-out procedures, they only work if the child WANTS to be in the activity that you are removing him from, or wants your attention. Taking a child out of circle for inappropriate behaviors could be his way of saying "Take me out of circle!" Putting a child that is reinforced by being alone, in time-out is not effective. Again, look at function before you use this or other techniques.

4) Over-correction and positive practice are great choices (having the child practice the behavior repeatedly and correctly until independence is established). These allow the child to immediately respond appropriately and correctly in a situation, allowing him/her to leave the situation on a positive note.

5) Response cost. This system is a variation on a token economy and works well for children who really like token systems and can handle delayed reinforcement. This system removes a token each time the target (inappropriate) behavior occurs, and the child must have a certain number (pre-determined) of tokens left to gain access to the reinforcer. This system can be extremely effective, but

| Module 4 | Strategies for Teaching Self Awareness *(continued)* |

also very upsetting to some children. Be careful to evaluate whether or not your child is ready to handle a system such as this.

Strategies for long-term planning:

○ It can be helpful to introduce the child to a simple way of "interrupting" their maladaptive behavior pattern and begin to self-monitor their own behaviors. This can serve as an easy to remember and quick on-the-spot strategy for everyday social situations. Here is an example: Stop, Look & Think/Change
We have used this strategy with many of our students and even had a visual made and posted in one of the first grade classrooms we visited. This phrase is repeated, like a "mantra" to encourage the child to "internalize" the procedure. Here's an example in practice: for one child it meant when he found himself (or the aide found him and cued him that he was doing "that target behavior") off-task, he was directed to "Stop, Look and Think/Change". "Stop what you're doing. Look at what the other kids were doing and Think/Change your plan of what to do or who to ask for help." This was expanded upon for older kids who were taught Stop, Look and Think when in social situations that had unclear social rules or was new to them. Stop-pause for a moment, Look at what other people are doing and find an appropriate model, and then Think about what to do next.

○ Self-monitoring systems can be very helpful, especially when tied in with natural reinforcement. Using a visual (picture or written) system can help a child to keep track of their own behavior and reward their efforts for remaining calm and responding appropriately. Checking in with your child, referencing pre-taught visuals and providing your child with written expectations and problem solving strategies can be very successful in increasing a child's independence. Note that these behaviors need to help your child to access reinforcement, or it needs to be provided for a "job well done".
* An example of some self-monitoring tools can be found in the Appendix.

○ Teaching relaxation techniques has had some success with children. This can be done in many ways, including the basic technique of teaching a child to ask for a "break" when it is needed, to more advanced techniques of teaching a child to become aware of when he/she is becoming stressed or anxious, what is triggering it, and to engage in a response that is appropriate, such as deep breathing or drawing. Be sure to keep in mind that an analysis of behavior is important here too, if a student is stressed and anxious and attempts to escape work, calming techniques will help, but determining why a student wants or needs to escape a

Module 4	**Strategies for Teaching Self Awareness** *(continued)*

behavior is important too.

○ Don't forget to work with both school and family on self-monitoring and good behavior. It is always helpful if school and home are working, in the same manner, to reinforce a child for demonstrating appropriate, desired behavior. Using a communication book, or meeting with the teacher(s) or parent(s) are effective ways of introducing the child's own self-monitoring methods.

○ Develop scripts and behavior expectations for different social events that can be practiced or rehearsed.

○ "Deconstruct" or carefully interpret social situations for children and give ideas on where to stand, where to look, what to do with their hands, how to excuse oneself politely, rehearse simple conversation topics and scripts, etc. Use the modules and teaching strategies in this manual.

○ Be sure that whatever technique you use, you name it and teach language with minimal cues from the teacher, parent or in the form of a visual cue, so the child can access it on his or her own.

Module 5: Conversation

Module 5 teaches how to acknowledge and respond to another persons' language or conversation thoughtfully, and to initiate and sustain conversations.

Adults and children use language for many reasons. A young child uses gestures and words to obtain desired items. The child imitates words he/she hears from his/her parents in search of social approval. As the child grows, language is used to ask and answer questions. As adults, language is used to share ideas, beliefs and thoughts and to establish and maintain many different relationships.

There are many skills required to have a conversation. Consider this: when we're having a conversation, we listen to the tone and intonation of the voice, we acknowledge a person's facial expressions, we place those in context to the words being said and we further analyze and interpret any "hidden meanings" (idioms, irony, etc,). We observe body language and posturing, and consider what we know about that person and the current situation. In short, we are receiving a LOT of communicative messages. We synthesize the information instantaneously, and formulate just as complicated and intricate a response to the other person. We do all of this generally without even being conscious of it!

Now think about the child with ASD. The child has to remember to look at the person, listen to the words, and make sense of all the subtly changing facial expressions and body language. As if that's not hard enough, he/she has to listen to the voice intonation and determine its meaning. All this, while trying to generate a related, on-topic verbal response, even if the topic is not particularly interesting to the child, or the conversation has interrupted his/her favorite activity. The child has to acknowledge the person speaking, then deliver his/her response in a timely manner, while maintaining eye contact, and then (voila!) your child is engaged in a conversation…Whew! This level of skill is so demanding, it's not hard to imagine how overwhelming it may be for the child who does not possess the skills necessary to do this at even the most basic level.

It is because of these complexities that it is very important to teach conversation by breaking it down into easily learned steps and using a systematic approach, with appropriate prompting and effective reinforcers. It is essential that the necessary skills be taught by building increased expectations on the solid foundation of mastered prerequisite skills. Having previously established joint attention skills and play skills in Modules 1 and 3, your child will now have greater opportunity to talk to his/her peers and will have something to talk about! Mastery of conversation skills for a child with ASD will enable them to converse and interact socially with greater ease. Using a compilation of mastered skills will minimize frustration and decrease negative or inappropriate behaviors. All of which will result in a more socially active child.

In order to learn any skill, a child must have the capacity for imitation (as taught in Module 1). Once the child can imitate words, he/she must consider the function of those words. In our example above, we noted that in the complicated conversation process, the child may have to answer on a topic that is not of particular interest. It is important to understand to a typically developing child the use of language and the accompanying social interaction is as reinforcing for them as it is for adults. For a child with ASD, these social interactions generally are NOT initially as reinforcing. Therefore, we need to make the use of language and conversation reinforcing by using strong and meaningful reinforcers. In other words, we must pair language with reinforcement, even if it's initially "outside the realm of natural contingencies" by using tokens, stickers, treats, or anything else that will help engage your child in conversation.

We would be remiss if we did not spend some time talking about the teachings of B.F. Skinner and his landmark book Verbal Behavior, 1957. In this book, Skinner writes a detailed analysis of how we functionally use "verbal behavior", how we are reinforced for using language. In addition, it provides important information regarding our language, that we use language to convey many things, that one word can have multiple functions and provide different levels of reinforcement. Using an ABA approach, this is important when teaching language.

It also is important for us to note some of the most basic terms coined by Skinner. This module is not designed to comprehensively teach verbal behavior philosophy or protocol, and all readers are encouraged to read more on this topic in other texts for further reference. This section is designed, however, to simplify and integrate the important work of Skinner into a social skills context.

Mand is a verbal behavior term for "request" that yields its own reinforcer. In other words, the function of the mand is to specify wanted items, or more simply, to make a request. Starting a functional communication program with teaching mands or requests is the first skill in the conversation module of the Social Skill Checklist. It's an important place to start because it teaches the child that use of language is reinforcing and it gets you what you want.

Tact is a verbal behavior term that refers to nouns, verbs, pronouns, adjectives, etc. It is commonly thought of as "labeling". Most language programs start here. It is important to hold teaching tacts until many mands are established. Make sure your labels are common items/events relevant to your child's life.

The intraverbal is answering other's questions, it is commenting on an action you are doing, and talking about something that did or will happen in the future. It is singing a song, reciting a poem or talking about something that is important to you. Intraverbals are often the most challenging to teach a child with autism who is not socially reinforced. Therefore careful attention to powerful reinforcers is imperative—as well as keeping the child successful with short interactions and appropriate prompting strategies.

The strategies listed here build basic prerequisite language skills, including imitation, simple requests/mands, and a repertoire of mastered tacts/labels. Strategies for building conversation skills, beginning with that foundation are listed below.

Module 5	**Strategies for Teaching Conversation**

- Use the Social Skill Checklist to determine your child's baseline level and goals.
- Don't underestimate the power of pairing reinforcement (praise, attention, tokens, treats, etc.) with the student's language in your teaching! Be specific and generous in your reinforcement, especially for students who are not inherently socially motivated.

Module 5 Strategies for Teaching Conversation *(continued)*

○ Teach beginning conversation by establishing that your child can answer "Yes/ No" questions. These are the simplest kind of questions to ask and answer.

○ Teach basic social questions, (intraverbals) such as "What is your name, age, birthday, etc". This can be taught by setting up visuals of the answer "My name is Daniel". Teach the correct response to your child using a visual prompt when needed. Slowly fade your visual (example, flash it, and then hide it as the child begins to respond) until your child can answer independently.

○ Once you have a child who has language skills beyond answering basic "Yes/No" and social questions move on to answering "WH" questions, such as "who" "what" "where" and then onto "why" and "when".

○ Work on general commenting. Have your child look around the room and name things that he/she sees "I see a fish!" Expand this to naming something he/she sees others doing or something others have "Jack has a new toy!", and finally to something that he/she is doing "I am going to the zoo". Each response should be reinforced, working up to giving points or rewards at any time of the day!

○ Three part conversation:
  • Greeting   • Comment   • Goodbye
  Start with a simple script, and then add in generalized language (generate several ways to say hello, goodbye or to get someone's attention). A sample script for a beginning three part conversation is:
  • **Greeting:** *"Hi!"*
  • **Statement/Comment:** *"I have that toy!"*
  • **Closing:** *"Gotta go, see you later!"*

○ You can then add in more language and question asking to the comment part of the equation. Keep in mind that the conversation is best if it is short and successful. Teaching questions and in-depth conversation skills to a child who has very poor eye contact and can't stand still is not appropriate. Having the student be successful with several shorter conversations will be more reinforcing and may help to build your child's confidence. Also, a short, sweet, successful conversation reduces the likelihood of errors and inappropriate behaviors, and will make peers or conversation partners more likely to engage your child in conversation again at another time.

○ Expand conversation skills by using a conversation flowchart to teach individual parts of the conversation process: greeting, ask a question about what they are doing, comment, say goodbye.

Module 5	**Strategies for Teaching Conversation** (continued)

- Once a child has more fluency in his basic conversation repertoire, teach the child to attend to and respond to your questions (contingent statements). There are teaching strategies below:

- It often helps to start off teaching social conversations by having a child answer more expanded questions (as language has developed). Choosing a topic of interest to your child is a great way to get started. Set the number of responses required if you have a "reluctant conversationalist". Explain to your child that you want them to answer 2 questions (gradually increasing the number of questions based on his/her success). Visually mark off each exchange for a clear ending to the task.

- Using a favorite video or computer game, pause it and ask questions allowing your child to answer and/or to comment spontaneously. Generalize this to imaginative play such as playing with trains or dolls or books, then to a siblings sports game or one on TV.

- Teach your child to pay compliments to others. You may prompt using visual cards to model compliments, or to signal when to compliment. You may prompt using a question such as "What do you think of Jack's new toy?"

- Teach your child to make contingent/topic statements. Teacher or peer says: "I like to eat pizza!" cue child to say "I like to eat hot dogs!"—the statement the child says in response is on topic (favorite things to eat) and related to the initial statement of the partner.

- Start your child playing the "word game"; name things in a category, to be sure he/she can stay on topic. Next, make a statement about something you like: You say, "I like cake", child comments, agreeing ("Me too!") or disagreeing ("I don't like that, but I do like (item)". Do this with things for which you have to get topic maintenance going. For example, things at the zoo, favorite foods, favorite movies, things to do after school, etc.

- Asking and answering questions. This refers to teaching the student to respond to everyday social situations and politeness. Learning appropriate responding to "What is that?" or "What are you doing?" Opening and/or holding the door for someone, asking "Are you okay" after someone gets hurt, asking, "What's wrong? What happened?" Saying "Bless you" after a sneeze, etc. Practice these one on one, and then generalize them into peer conversation.

- Teach your child to inquire about others likes and dislikes. We recommend teaching your child to list some of his/her favorite things and then ask others if they like them too. Expand this to general topic lists: favorite movies, favorite foods, favorite toys, etc. (Start with visual cards if your child needs help listing.)

- Teach your child how to interrupt, and the nuances involved in this:

| Module 5 | Strategies for Teaching Conversation *(continued)* |

– when there are two of you, wait until the person is done

– when there is more then one person, wait until a natural pause occurs and use interjections, such as "Excuse me."

– when you are in school, you need to raise your hand first

Teach this by modeling or role playing.

Read on for some helpful prompting ideas:

○ Video modeling can be very helpful as a teaching strategy. Videotape each of the above activities as a way to introduce each step. If your child has difficulty, you may need to supplement the video with written or picture visual supports to show what you expect in each step. Additionally, a tally sheet can be set up to record the number of steps you want your child to complete, so he/she will know when the task (which may be difficult or non-preferred) is over. Don't forget to keep reinforcing attempts and correct responses! This is hard work for your child and the more positive the experience the more likely your child will keep trying and eventually have success.

○ Practice, preview and rehearsal strategies can be extremely effective when working on conversation skills. Review expectations in the form of social stories, social schedules, and role play before interacting with peers.

○ Create a book about the child's friends with pictures and an "interview" form as a way of promoting social interaction, and also finding common interests that can lead to reinforcing play or conversation opportunities. An example of this type of book is provided in the appendix.

○ Remember to teach the child appropriate times to start conversations (lunch or recess, not when the teacher is talking) and with whom to insure maximum success and opportunity for reciprocity. Having conversation starters in a small notebook for the child to refer to can be helpful.

○ Create scenarios to role-play, that could happen at school. By teaching your child responses to situations, he/she will be more prepared, and therefore more likely to engage in conversation.

○ Conversation Role Play

What's happening:

You are in the cafeteria.

You do not know anyone at your table.

A boy you don't know sits down next to you

You Say:

"_____"

Module 5	Strategies for Teaching Conversation *(continued)*

- Teach your child good conversation endings, such as "Okay, see ya later" or "It was nice chatting with you" or "I gotta go now" or "OK, bye". Then teach your child how to tell when the conversation is over by recognizing a pause, a downward glance or a shift in eye gaze or realizing he/she has nothing else to say.

Module 6: Perspective Taking

Module 6 teaches your child the ability to label and interpret other's emotions, show compassion to others and change behavior as appropriate.

Children with autism often have significant difficulty interpreting social cues, understanding that there is another person's viewpoint, and then ascertaining what it might be. This step in learning social cues is often referred to as 'perspective taking'. It may be very difficult for a child with autism to understand that other people may feel differently then they do, that others may have different experiences and different opinions. Often linked to this is the term "theory of mind", which refers to the ability to recognize that other people have thoughts and feelings separate from ours. Most people learn this skill by watching the people around them and from the empathetic responses of our parents. We also observe and imitate others, the beginning of which was taught in Module 1!

Encompassing the process of perspective taking is the abilities to recognize and interpret other people's emotions, provide empathy (the ability to "put yourself in another's shoes") and perhaps, as needed, change behavior in response to the interpretation of what someone is feeling and their response to you.

However challenging these concepts can be for us, they are necessary for successful social interaction and therefore, an important component in the social skills learning process.

There is an excellent book on this subject listed in our resources called Reaching Out, Joining In, Teaching Social Skills to Young Children with Autism, by Mary Jane Weiss, Ph.D. and Sandra L. Harris, Ph.D. In this book the authors take time to list some prerequisite skills that should be in place prior to including perspective as a target skill. These include:

- Language Skills: a strong receptive language repertoire including, yes/no, I/you, and "Wh" questions,

○ Social Skills: accurately identify emotions in stories, emotions in self and others in context (not just on flashcards and contrived situations), and multiple emotions-beyond happy, sad, angry, surprised
○ Social responses, including politeness markers
○ Understanding real vs. pretend

We now refer back to our basic ABA principles of determining your child's goal (what skill you will be teaching), breaking it into discrete steps, outlining expectations clearly so that the child understands what is expected, and using reinforcement procedures and generalization programming to ensure that the skills taught are skills learned and used.

Module 6	Strategies for Teaching Perspective

○ Use the Social Skills Checklist to determine your child's baseline level and goals.
○ A good starting place is identifying emotions. Teaching your child to label emotions (first receptively then expressively) in pictures is the starting point of a multi-faceted emotion recognition/awareness skill program. After mastery of pictures, move on to imitation of emotions by your child, then to identifying other people's (sibling's or teacher's) imitations.
○ Play charades with emotions. Pick an emotion, and then act it out, using face and body gestures. Use visuals if necessary to help your child model this, but quickly fade the visual. Another method you could try is video taping various students acting out various emotions to teach your child to identify and imitate what he/she sees. Expand on this by playing charades in which a student or peer acts out an action that led to the emotion and have your child guess both the action and emotion. For example, falling and then crying. Expand this to a group activity.
○ This one is from the Reaching Out, Joining In, field of vision tasks. Teach your child to understand that others might not see what he/she sees. Sit your child and his/her peer back to back, facing opposite directions. You or the teacher can start by naming items that your child can't see. Say, "I see this, can you?" Then each child takes a turn, naming what he/she can see. Review why one can see and the other can't. Expand on this theme, have two children/students in the room, place item(s) in a container. Have one child leave the room and the other stay. Once the item(s) is removed, have your child re-enter room. Instruct your child to retrieve the item(s) from the container, but he/she obviously won't find it. Have the other child show where the item(s) is now hidden, and say, "I know where it is because I saw where it was hidden". Repeat this with your child seeing

| Module 6 | **Strategies for Teaching Perspective** (continued) |

the item and helping the other child find it. Review why your child would look in the place it was originally hidden.

○ Expand on the above strategy with puppets, or with two peers while your child watches. Act out a story, where one puppet or child sees something that the other does not. Review what happened to hidden item(s).

○ Teach your child to look at others, and recognize some of their attributes, hair color, clothing color, eye color, glasses or no glasses. To expand this, make up your own "guess who" game with peers. Teach your child to recognize features of others first. "Guess who's wearing a blue shirt?" Then "guess who's happy, sad etc"

○ Play "twenty questions", in which your child has 20 questions to guess the object you're thinking of. If prompting is necessary, provide questions verbally or written on cards. Start with obvious, visible objects and then move to objects not visibly present to make it more challenging.

○ To teach higher level skills, such as recognizing emotions, and WHY others feel emotions, use video modeling of cause and effect (film a situation and the appropriate emotion). Possible situations include getting a present and being happy, or being sad because it's raining and you can't go out to play. Social stories are additional effective tools.

○ Making observations. Have children present their favorite toys, and see who has the same toys, and who has different toys. Expand this to family photos: Using family pictures and vacation photos have your child observe who has brothers and sisters, where his/her peers went, and how people are the same and different, observing attributes.

○ Books in which the characters are particularly animated can be used for observing social cues in the environment and possible reasons for emotion. Instead of reading the text, tell the story through the pictures. If in the picture the dog is running...and the boy has an upset look on his face and his arms are up in the air... describe the action, how does the boy feel? Describe the nonverbal language in the pictures, what emotion is he/she feeling based on this gesture? Your child can act out the picture or act out what he/she would do if he/she were in this situation.

○ Playing a video without the volume can be used in a similar manner. Pause it and talk about the expressions on people's faces, what environmental cues are present, and what could have happened to cause it.

○ Set up videos of "correct play" scenarios (kids being nice to each other, kids playing with toys the right way) and "incorrect play" scenarios (kids being mean

Module 6	Strategies for Teaching Perspective *(continued)*

to each other, kids yelling and interrupting). Have your child identify right and wrong and act out the correct ways that were observed.

○ Teach a child to label emotions on others, and have your child ask that other person "WHY" they are feeling this way. Video modeling of students asking others how they feel will work well as a prompt. We made a video of different emotions, children going up and asking the child why they were happy or sad. After we showed this video to some children on the spectrum, they began to ask the question "Why are you crying" to a classmate that cried during the day.

○ Look at how others have different points of view. Start off simple by hiding something in your pocket or in a box. Explain to your child that "I" know what's in the box, but "you" don't because "you" can't see it. Make it fun by giving clues as to what it is. Take turns by having your child hide something that you don't see, and talk about why you can't find it.

○ Teach a child how to help others. This goes along way towards beginning to empathize with others. Teach an opening phrase, such as "I can help you" or "let me try". Start simply by unsuccessfully trying to do something your child can do easily. Prompt the child to recognize that you need help using exaggerated facial expressions or openly discussing your struggle. If your child doesn't use the previously taught phrase ("I can help you"), prompt by asking for help. Watch videos or role-play other scenarios where children may need help and another child offers assistance. Help generalize this to other parts of the school day and home.

○ Begin teaching your child to look around his/her home or classroom and point out other's emotions and the social cues that may be causing them.

○ Teach your child some social politeness markers and empathy to others once he/she recognizes the emotions, such as: offering help, saying excuse me, apologizing, asking if someone is OK, offering/providing assistance, and stopping a behavior in response to another child's facial expression.

○ You can use video modeling or video feedback as a method to help teach the child these skills.

○ Help teach a child about shared/not-shared experiences, to gain a sense that others may have different experiences. This can be done by starting out making lists or drawings of who likes what: listing or drawing likes and dislikes and comparing and sharing them. Have many children group together based on their likes and dislikes. Make it a game: all children that like candy, line up here, all children that don't like candy, line up here! Switch from topic to topic, based on favorite movies, pets, games, TV. shows, etc.

| **Module 6** | **Strategies for Teaching Perspective** *(continued)* |

○ Help the child by providing and reviewing visual support of the social rules. You may need to teach specific skills, such as keeping hands to self, staying in line, not interrupting, not stealing toys, etc.

○ Teach nonverbal communication and gestural and body cues. Label body signals to advanced emotions (anxious, frustrated, impatient, etc.). Then teach the child appropriate responses to these emotions.

○ Teach an advanced level of offering help. There are 3 levels to offering help: 1) serious injury, 2) emotional help, 3) someone lifting, carrying, and opening. Teach the appropriate response to each situation. It may help to initially teach with video modeling for each level. Then role-play with a visual reminder of each step.

○ Teach children to suspend their judgment and say "I don't know", when they are not in a position to know. This is an important skill.

○ Teach the skill of gently correcting others. Many times children with autism like to be right, and correct others or remind others of the rules. Set-up self-monitoring charts to help the student (either eliminate the correcting, or replace with more appropriate strategies to correct).

○ Once your child can identify and imitate emotions, use strategies to explore possible REASONS for the emotions. Have your child create a feelings book, a sort of journal, where he/she writes or draws his/her emotions in context. For example, your child gets kicked while walking in front of a swing, have him/her draw a picture of what happened and how it made him/her feel. This book could be used after the child exhibits a particular emotion as a means of identifying and working through his/her emotional state.

Module 7: Critical Thinking

Many children with autism have amazing rote memory abilities. They are able to recall events and recite facts second to none. However, as we discussed earlier, their ability to integrate that information, and to relate it to something else or to arrive at a new thought or idea can be extremely difficult. These skills refer to "higher order" thinking, and they are frequently a challenge to the student with autism.

Critical thinking allows us to (1) recognize that we need to evaluate a situation in the first place (2) plan how to evaluate it, using specific resources and techniques (3) apply the techniques to the situation, and then, (4) engage in a meta-cognitive thought processes to evaluate the situation and our actions/thoughts about it, and then (5) self-correct if necessary with no outside prompting.

Problem solving skills allow us to create options to resolve or respond to a dilemma. These skills come from the ability to recognize the components of a problem and then integrate those individual components into a solution that reflects our beliefs and priorities.

Executive functioning skills allow us to decide on an activity, create a plan to accomplish it, and follow through, gathering the necessary materials and staying focused until the task is complete.

These skills are a challenge for many typical students and general education classrooms nationwide are working to deliberately address these skills in everyday lesson planning. In programming for students with autism, the challenge becomes even greater because to teach these skills, we rely on language and symbolic and relative relationships, not factual, concrete or rote information. In fact, creativity is required because two similar problems may require two very different solutions.

Neurology is also at work here, especially in executive functioning skills. Frontal lobe and right hemisphere functioning is directly related to impaired deficits in these areas. Learning these skills becomes a matter of creating new brain pathways and acquiring compensatory strategies, in other words, learning a new way to solve an old problem rather than going down the same path and getting stuck each time.

Kathy Quill writes on this subject as well, in her book, Do-Watch-Listen-Say. She notes that "In general, (children with autism have) difficulties with integration of information, abstract reasoning, and cognitive flexibility". She takes this a step further, to state, "cognitive processing is a multi-layer system in which information is analyzed, organized, stored, and remembered in complex ways. A person instantly links a new experience to a number of past related experiences".

Looking at this, from our cognitive breakdown above, and the research done thus far, we see that this process of linking experiences does not occur in the same manner for children with autism. We are reminded of Temple Grandin and her insight into how, (instead of this process), she "thinks in pictures". Thus, it is important not to be frustrated with the child with autism that can't problem solve what to do in a situation, or cannot possibly understand the important meaning in a story. These skills need to be broken down and systematically taught.

Module 7	Teaching Strategies for Critical Thinking

- ○ Use the Social Skill Checklist to determine your child's baseline level and goals.
- ○ Teaching the concept: "First this, then that" is actually a first step toward teaching problem solving. This concept helps a child to delay an immediate desire (reinforcer), as well as to understand beginning sequencing of events in a natural context. This can often be taught with a visual board and picture schedule. Set up "First" (picture of blocks), "Then" (picture of Playdoh). It is helpful to teach this concept first with two items that are of equal value to the child, so that the situation feels calm and easy to manage. Then build up to putting a less desired task "First" before a more preferred task second, to teach delay of reinforcement and sequencing.
- ○ Teach basic problem solving with visual help to organize. Start with a basic problem, building a paper bag puppet, for example. Provide the necessary tools. Teach your child to organize what's needed first, second, etc. (like a sequencing goal). Lay out the objects with corresponding numbers. 1) the bag, 2) the markers, etc. Expand this to next teach the child to find what he/she needs to make the object, and lay out the items with their corresponding numbers, and then start the project, independently. Advance this to higher-level problem solving: such as making a list of items or putting together items needed for a trip, or for school, teaching the child to sequence and organize his/her day and needs.
- ○ Teach your child to listen to and then re-tell a story. Break the story down visually, set up visual categories such as characters (use pictures), what they are doing (pictures of actions), where they are going and what happens at the end. Teach a child by first slowly going through the story and writing down each category as it happens, or using Mayer-Johnson pictures to represent each section, and categorize it. Then your child can re-tell the story, following the pictures. With success, fade the pictures, and use the pictures happening in the storybook itself or have your child re-tell the story from memory.
- ○ Visual memory: remembering objects/pictures that are held up. It is helpful to teach your child how to "echo back to themselves" what they saw as a rehearsal strategy (like we do as adults when we are trying to remember a phone number). This short-term memory skill can be very helpful. Do this by showing one picture (of a known object) and then another picture (of a known object) and teach the child to say aloud what he/she sees as they are seeing it. Immediately ask what they saw, the child should be able to recite back, from the rehearsal strategy. Next, delay the time between presenting the objects and asking what the child saw. Increase this memory skill, with more picture objects, then with auditory words instead of pictures.

| Module 7 | **Teaching Strategies for Critical Thinking** (continued) |

- Identify differences, ask "What is different?" in pictures. Ask "What is wrong?" by using worksheets found in critical thinking workbooks. Good resources include No Glamour Language or Social Skills Activities for Secondary Students with Special Needs (see Resource section).

- Identify objects by exclusion, find the ones that are not present. This can be a difficult concept for children. With graphic organizers, set up visually, items that are the same, and then pick the one that's not the same.

- Teach your child to make lists of things he/she needs for various events and organize them around themes: what happens at night vs. what happens in the morning. This can be done visually with pictures or words. This is beginning problem solving, and can then be expanded.

- Use delays and pauses to encourage your child to problem solve. For instance, if you spill milk, ask "Hmmm, now what should we do?" Or, if there is a point in a story that the character needs to make a decision, ask "What would be some choices for __?" If your child is not able to do this, then you will need to teach the response to these situations. You may need to start by visually organizing the problems. For instance, 1) have a picture of spilled milk, 2) have a picture of the milk cleaned, 3) help the child determine how did the milk get cleaned up. If the child cannot do this, create sequenced pictures and have the child sequence them and describe them. Then, take out different steps of the sequence and have your child describe the step that should be there. Take it further and then act out the story in the sequence cards, have your child now get a rag and clean the milk.

- In this category, being able to listen to directions and follow-through is important. Children are faced with this every day in school, they're given a set of directions, with choices provided by the teacher. Teach your child to listen and follow directions (use visuals or make notes), and make decisions and follow-through. Once a system is taught, your child will go far in school.

- Teach your child to check a variety of sources to confirm or reject opinions or viewpoints.

- Teach your child to build in flexibility. Start off simple by setting a visual schedule for your child, and then, at some point in the day, make a change, use a visual card that says, "Change". Then substitute one activity, for an equally preferred activity, so it is not too challenging. Gradually, make different changes in the day adding more and more challenging changes.

Module 8: Advanced Language

Children with autism often experience tremendous difficulties in social language and the expansive world of pragmatics. Kelly once asked a student what it meant to "fall in love", and he very honestly told her, "it is when you hold hands, kiss, and fall down". He told her literally what that expression meant to him. Children with autism think in very literal, concrete terms. Another child told Kelly that when "it is raining cats and dogs" it means that "it is raining and the cats are hitting the dogs because the cats don't like the rain". Although comical, it made us think how difficult it must be to understand conversation and all of the social nuances that go with our language. What may happen is that these children excel in areas with factual and procedural information. In these other, more abstract language skill areas, they are less successful and the gap between typical peers and the child with autism widens.

As with the other skills that are taught systematically, these higher-level language skills have to be "broken down" into manageable parts and taught for functional use. As the child grows older and matures, it is important that the learning environment and the goals of what to teach be meaningful and useful. This includes teaching the child to interpret body language and social cues that are relevant to their lives. This includes teaching language pragmatic skills such as white lies, idioms and homonyms that are relevant to their lives.

Module 8 | Strategies for Teaching Advanced Language

- Have your speech and language pathologist or behavior specialist do an assessment on language pragmatics to determine important areas of need. This can be an important area for a team approach. Utilizing special education services, classroom teachers and speech and language pathologists to coordinate these skills will be the most successful approach.
- Teach body language and interpreting non-verbal cues. It can be fun to start off with using your body for meaning first, such as playing charades.
- Teach body interpreting by using videos children like. Try using a video, turning off the volume and pausing it and asking what emotions a person is showing based on body language. Turn on the volume and watch it again to see if the words match the body language.
- Write out several index cards with an emotion or situation on each one (sad, frustrated, in a hurry, tired, anxious, proud, etc.) Lay the cards on the table in an array of 2 to 20. Take turns acting one out and having your child try to guess which card it is. Notice how the "acting" of the child with autism may be grand

Module 8	Strategies for Teaching Advanced Language *(continued)*

or overt and "over-acted" compared to your more subtle gestures, etc. Make a note of this to the child and then work with the child on recognizing more subtle cues from people, and how to communicate with "smaller" non-verbal communication signals.

○ Teach higher level social pragmatics such as jokes and idioms BUT only after other above social skills are in place. Use visuals for this.

○ Look at worksheets and visuals to teach other advanced level skills, such as para-phrasing, inferences, homonyms, and metaphors. Use the necessary visuals and skills breakdown to teach these skills. Don't forget to then generalize them into stories and into the school day.

○ Teach the child how to find the main idea of a story. A lot of times our children hear the words, but then are not able to summarize main ideas of the story. Worksheets from Teach Me Language can be very helpful, as they help the child to slowly breakdown the story, by looking at characters, actions, end results, and then you can add in emotions/feelings of characters. This will help also when listening to conversations.

○ Teach the child to make introductions. Again, videotaping this process, and using written scripts can be effective tools.

○ Teach the child how to interject or hold onto the conversation (and then… "can you believe it? that's cool!")

○ Sponge Bob Square Pants ® is a popular cartoon right now, and is chock full of inferences, hidden meanings, slang and idioms. Watch this and break down all of these, while having fun with your child.

○ Break down non-verbal communication into zones: face, arms, legs, space, etc. Facial expressions can be broken down even further into three more "zones" eyes, nose, and mouth and cheeks. Teach the child to recognize each zone and what messages each zone can tell you in different situations. For example, someone rolling their eyes, someone checking their watch, tapping their fingers, smiling, grinding their teeth, scratching their nose, and what each one means.

○ Teach the child advanced use of contingent statements, commenting on another person's comment, a "volleyball" of conversation. One way to do this is to use visuals and an actual ball. Sit at a table and start off with a topic: "I went to the beach today" Roll the ball to the student, and help them comment on your state-ment (you may need to provide visual scripts for this, such as "I like the beach" or "I played at the park today." To keep the conversation rolling, roll the ball back and forth. The person with the ball needs to comment on the other person's

| Module 8 | Strategies for Teaching Advanced Language *(continued)* |

conversation. Add in peers. Then, fade out the ball for a more natural conversation, generalize to recess, lunch and other natural opportunities.

○ Video the students having a conversation. Spend time reviewing and making corrections, etc, as a form of video feedback.

○ To help your child practice putting all of the conversation pieces together, role-play different scenarios that might be common in school. For example, have your child pick a friend, and a topic, such as an upcoming field trip. Now, work with your child to role-play what he/she might say in a conversation with another child. Having ready comments and questions will help your child to feel more comfortable, and therefore more likely to exhibit the conversation skills you are hoping for.

○ Work with your child, put reminder cards of comments, questions, and topic initiators that could be used in his/her lunch bag, or back pack. The child's teacher or support person should then help the child review the cards at the start of each day, or before lunch and or recess, or other social opportunities.

A great resource list of conversational messages can be found at www.lburhart.com/chat_ideas.htm

Module 9: Friendship

What makes a friendship? This is a question we posed to ourselves. We thought it would be helpful to further develop the idea of a friendship and what this means to our students and your child. We wanted to try and teach the concept of friendship not just as a series of behaviors and responses, but also as a relationship. To quote Webster's dictionary, the root word, relate, means "to connect or associate, as in thought or meaning; to show sympathetic understanding and awareness…"

 We asked some children, both neurotypical children and children with autism, about their thoughts on friendship. Here is what they said in response to our questions:
- ○ "What is a friend?"
- ○ "What do you do with a friend?"
- ○ "How do you know if someone is your friend?"

Joey (Age 5, ASD*) *"A friend is someone that I run and play with."*

Alex (Age 6, ASD*) *"You play."* (Play what?) *"You play."*

Sarah (Age 5, ASD*) *"I don't know, they come to my house."*

Jay (10, HFA*) *"A friend is a faithful person who tells the truth and never lies." "You hang out together and talk and play. You do things that you like." "If they are nice to you and don't take advantage of you."*

Kyle (8, ASD) *"Well, I don't know what a friend is. So you tell me and then I'll learn" "It's of playing with." "Well, like at school, at recess, I play with them and then I have a great time."*

Andrew (12, ASD*) *"Someone you play with." "You play!" "You're nagging—Janis, how do I shut this off!?" "I don't know."*

Kate (Age 7, NT*) *"It's someone you like and you like to play with them." "I just walk with them a lot, sit with them at lunch, play with them at recess, talk with them at recess. Sometimes, they stare at you and their face just gives it away that they like you. And then you think, oh, ok, she likes me."*

Ben (Age 7, NT*) *"A friend is someone who is fun to play with and you like them and you like to play games with them. You play with them and um, you invite each other over for play dates and they're fun. If they like you a lot and they want to play with you a lot and invite you over a lot and talk to you a lot."*

(**ASD: Autism Spectrum Disorder, HFA: High Functioning Autism, NT: Neurotypical*)

Friendships and autism

When we look at the comments from the children we interviewed on friendship, it is interesting to note several key components of friends that the neurotypical children mention:

- Play with them
- Talk
- Lunch
- Have fun
- Play dates

- Play games
- Recess
- "Look at their face" (non-verbal cues)
- Reciprocal invitations to one another's home

The neurotypical children were able to label many different attributes of friendships. Some were even able to assimilate verbal and non- verbal cues to determine partner's state of mind, thoughts or feelings.

The children with autism had a slightly more difficult time, mostly describing play as the only attribute (a developmentally younger version of a friend), and some became slightly agitated at our questions about this topic. So what does this mean when trying to teach the idea of friends and friendships to children with autism?

After working with some very talented and intelligent children with autism, we have come to understand that the skill of social interest and making friends needs to be specifically taught—the good news is that it can be. However this desire to have friends or to be liked by others may not be intrinsic for a child with autism.

Of relevance, Wing and Gold (1979) divided atypical social interactions occurring in the spectrum of autistic disorders into three broad types (a) aloof, (b) passive, and (c) active but odd. The aloof group corresponds more closely to the hallmark images of autism. This group comprises, by definition, children and adults who are most cut off from social contacts. They may become agitated when in close proximity to others, make unusual comments, and reject unsolicited physical or social contacts. However, for a brief period of time, they may enjoy some physical play.

From this literature perspective, we must look at the social skill needs and motivations of each child. We must make sure and teach the necessary progression of social skills that will bring them closer to a friendship, hopefully reaching a satisfying relationship.

We have had many parents tell us that although they were happy with the play skills being taught to their child, what they really wanted was for their child to have a friend, go to a birthday party, or be asked for a play-date after school. They wanted their child to want to be with friends and to enjoy their friends. Our answer is that it can happen, but it first involves the teaching of the certain skills in order for these opportunities to become available to the child.

Module 9	Strategies for Developing Friendships

○ Find other children that share a similar interest as your child, and live close by. Or, if there is a sibling, spend time teaching the siblings to play one or two things well. Pick Legos, Pokemon cards, or other activities that they could do without "killing each other", either parallel, or as a joint activity. Reinforce both children highly for this successful play.

○ Setting up play dates can be a good way to make friends. If you pair your child up with lots of fun activities, other children will want to be with your child. It is often helpful to structure these play dates and plan carefully, to help them go well. Set up a visual schedule and practice with the child first. Keep play dates short at first to ensure success. Here is a sample play date:
— Greet Friend
— Play games, or play joint game such as Legos/blocks
   (choose a game the child has learned to play well)
— Have a snack (set up conversation scripts/support)
— Play video games or watch a video
— Goodbye *see appendix for sample visual.

○ Expand play dates to birthday parties or sponsor a swim party.

○ Take friends to the movies. Practice going to movies first, then practice talking about the movie and favorite parts, using support scripts if necessary. This can be done first with parents and siblings and then other children, it may also be helpful to see the same movie twice.

○ Find peers that have similar interests and plan play dates with those peers.

○ Work on telephone skills. Try to start this teaching with video modeling of some telephone conversation. Then, set up practice conversations. Use a phone at home for the child and a cell phone for the conversation partner to start off looking at each other, and then slowly move distances and create more of an actual phone experience. Use scripts of what to say (asking a friend over, or calling for homework help) and practice pacing, waiting for the other to answer, etc. Then call other people to practice, such as grandparents. Then try calling your friends. Don't forget to practice scenarios including what to do if you get an answering machine, or if someone is not home. It can be helpful to have these 3

| **Module 9** | **Strategies for Developing Friendships** (continued) |

different situations available as scripts as you make the phone calls.

○ Teach the idea that friends like the same things. In a social skills group or a class, put two giant different colored hula-hoops or pieces of paper on the ground. Hold up signs of favorite topics, a movie, a food, a book, a TV show. Those that like that item, go to the red hula-hoop or paper. Those that don't, go to the green hula-hoop or paper. Then, within those groups, help the friends recognize that they like or don't like the same things. Use a visual. "We like the same thing" and "We don't like the same thing" can be a fun interactive activity that because of the motor movement promotes participation and attending.

○ Help the child to find other students that may have similar interest. Teach appropriate questions to ask about interests. Help foster that interest (appropriately) by helping the child to join clubs with the students, or start their own "club" at their house based on that interest.

○ Practice telling jokes. Simple jokes, or tongue twisters (use a written or picture copy to help the students) can be a fun way to promote language and get the fun rolling. There are websites for children's jokes, check on-line, also check the local library for joke books.

○ Use favorite videos that demonstrate friendships, and what makes a friend, including being nice, helping others, liking the same things, making each other laugh, etc.

○ Use worksheets, such as Darlene Mannix's book Social Skills Activities for Secondary Students. There are several sections in this workbook that have helpful skill builders such as: Ways to Make Friends worksheets.

○ Have your child make a "Friend" book. Add name and pictures of classmates and friends in the neighborhood, and list what your child likes about them, and what your child has in common. Plan play dates around these things.

○ Have a "welcome" to kindergarten or second grade, or camp party for your child. This will give you the opportunity to meet your child's peers and their parents and create some connections outside of the classroom. You may need to break it down by inviting only a few children at a time.

○ Use our best buddies program to help set up allies for your children. Many times a child with autism may be in a social situation that, despite the best teaching, they are not prepared to handle. An ally can help them through this, and support and protect the student if needed (see Appendix).

Module 10:   Community Skills

Having worked with many schools and families, we often hear, "my child has mastered so many academic areas, yet we can't go out in public as a family without having a major behavior problem". It is difficult for a family when the child doesn't know how to go to a restaurant properly, can't accompany a parent in the grocery store or simple errands, ignores the phone when it rings or answers it inappropriately, or doesn't know how to make a bed or clean their room. In short, it's the everyday life that happens with or without autism.

These life skills are important for both the family and child to live harmoniously. They are skills that don't come up as often at school, yet are vital to a child's real-life education and ability to function in the community. We include them in the social skills checklist so they are not forgotten. Sometimes it is simply a matter of good generalization. For example, a child may be taught to say "Hi" and look at his/her teacher or tutor in the classroom. Yet the child may not say "Hi" to his/her grandparent. A child may be taught to wait in line to go out to recess, yet can't wait in line at the grocery store with his/her mother. Many children can ride in the car with family, yet can't ride on the bus to go to a class field trip. Generalization is crucial!

It is important that life skills, safety skills and community skills be a component to every child's teaching program. Generally, if a school program is working diligently on academic and social skills, this area of life skills will require additional attention from the family. Some examples of skill areas to teach include:

Community Goals: The necessary skills to go out with their family, which may include going to restaurants, church, visiting family and friends, holiday gatherings, going to the mall and going to the grocery store, and other errands, successfully.

Daily Living Skills: The ability to independently dress, wear appropriate (and hopefully peer similar) clothing, make their own bed, do household chores and actively participate in home life.

Safety Skills: The necessary skills to be safe, may include:
○ Seeking out help if he/she/someone is hurt
○ Sidewalk and crosswalk safety, both alone and with family
○ Fire safety including alarm recognition and ability to exit
○ Calling 911, providing name, address and reason for the call

This is a short list. Look at the skills of your child and his/her daily needs to determine what skills are needed to function harmoniously at home and in the community. See the Social Skills Checklist for a comprehensive list to determine priority.

Module 10	Strategies for Teaching Community Skills

- ○ We can't say enough about the use of visuals/role-playing/video modeling to teach these skills. Once you have determined what skills you are going to teach, start out by framing each scenario visually. This could mean photographing each step and/or video modeling the scenario. First, establish your child's attention, simply go through the visual scenario. A sort of social story of what the situation is (ex, lining up in the cafeteria for lunch or what to do when the fire alarm goes off), and what you expect of your child. Reinforce even this level of attending. Next, watch videos of the desired responses (children on line and responding appropriately to the fire drill). *For fire safety tips and video clips see www.fema.gov/kids/v_lib.htm and http://safetypub.com/cfph/cfph.htm

- ○ Next, role-play the scenarios. Go through the exact responses, using visual supports. It's important to reinforce frequently to maintain interest and therefore increase the likelihood that your child will respond appropriately and repeatedly.

- ○ Practice-Practice-Practice. Set up as real to actual situations as possible. Preview the expectations early on, then later set up the scenario. Do this again, with an increasing delay in the preview of expectations and the situations, until none is used, yet you get the correct response. Reinforce!!!!

- ○ Visuals: Outline for the child in visual format the expectations of the trip—where you are going, what you will do, how will you know you are done, what the child will have to do, what the appropriate language and behavior responses are, etc.

- ○ Role-playing: Practice community trips at home by role playing them at home first, and preparing the child for what to expect, as well, as how to respond.

- ○ Gradual exposure: Do not plan to teach appropriate grocery story behavior when you have a large shopping list. Depending on the behaviors and baseline level of skills, plan to go to the grocery store when you have nothing you have to buy. Instead, first review the expectations, then just go to the store parking lot, maybe go to the doors, maybe even go inside, for just a moment, and then come back out again, and reinforce appropriate behaviors. Try again tomorrow. Each day, add a little to the time and response requirements, but keep it short and successful. Be prepared to go home at any point.

- ○ The same procedure can be used for church, shopping, local errands, going in the car, visiting relatives and friends, and practicing for holidays—well in advance of December! Perhaps start with the errands that are the least unpleasant.

| Module 10 | **Strategies for Teaching Community Skills** *(continued)* |

- ○ Video procedures as outlined in the video section of this manual can also be of great assistance for many students. We have mentioned this several times, but we really can't say enough about it.

- ○ Keep in mind that there are lots of new and unfamiliar stimuli in the community. Plan for this by providing increased support and realistic, appropriate expectations, to insure (as much as possible) the child's success. This is very important, frequently community outings have been difficult at best for families, so you may be confronted with a pattern of inappropriate behavior. Plan for this by figuring out what has been a trigger for behavior in the past and address that as a priority (hint—identify the trigger by functional analysis!!!).

Part 2

• • •

GETTING TO WORK

- Skills assessment samples

- Building a program from assessments

- Teaching social skills in school

- Tips for using peer buddies

- Tips for paraprofessionals

Conducting the Assessment

As practitioners, we are often asked to work with students on social skills. Here is a sample scenario:

Background

Timmy is a 5-year-old boy entering kindergarten. He was diagnosed with autism at 3 years old, and has had intensive ABA services provided to him by his school system both in school and at home. Timmy has made tremendous progress in the past 2 years, both academically and with language. He is near age-level with many academic skills; fine and gross motor, and near age-level with language. He can play with many toys.

Assessment

Timmy's program needs a comprehensive assessment. Timmy's school team decides to use both the Social Behavior Assessment Inventory, as well as our Social Skills Checklist.

Using our Social Skills Checklist, Level 1, the team was able to determine that although Timmy had made great gains thanks to years of intensive teaching, he still had many areas of need socially. From the Social Skills Checklist, the following skills were determined to be areas of need:

 # The Social Skills Checklist — Level 1

Student: _____TIMMY_____	Yes/No 1:1	Yes/No In Group	Yes/No Natural Setting
Module 1: Joint Attention/Attending			
Looks when called/comes when called	Yes	Yes	Yes
Turns and orients toward person when making requests	Yes	Yes	Yes
"Follows eye gaze, point or gesture by others"	Yes	Yes	Yes
Looks/orients/responds to object presented	Yes	Yes	Yes
Looks/orients when listening to others (shifts body/ gaze every few sec.)	Yes	No	No
Imitates 1-2 step motor tasks	Yes	Yes	Yes
Looks expectantly for something to happen	Yes	Yes	Yes
Sits and attends to simple tasks (10 min)	Yes	No	No
Sits quietly in circle	NA	Yes	Yes
Imitates hand movements in circle	NA	Yes	Yes
Calls out in unison	NA	No	No
"Follows basic 1,2 step auditory directions (directed at group)"	NA	Yes	Yes
Sits next to peers	NA	Yes	Yes
Passes item to peers	NA	No	No
Gains appropriate attention of others	Yes	Yes	Yes
Module 2 Greetings			
Waves	Yes	Yes	Yes
Says "Hi" in response to greetings	Yes	Yes	Yes
Walks up to others to greet	Yes	No	No
Says "Bye"	Yes	Yes	Yes
Politeness Marker			
Says "Please"	Yes	Yes	Yes
Reciprocates affection	Yes	Yes	Yes
Module 3 Social Play			
Sustains independent play for 15 min. w/close-ended toys i.e. puzzles	Yes	Yes	Yes
Plays parallel +15 minutes, close to peers w/close-ended toys	Yes	Yes	Yes
Plays with open ended toys i.e. blocks, trucks, legos (builds)	Yes	Yes	Yes
Imitates movement with objects	Yes	Yes	Yes
Imitates peers w/ peer leader in songs, Simon says, etc.	NA	Yes	Yes
Imitates up to 4-6 actions in play routines	Yes	Yes	Yes
Takes a turn for 5 turns w/concrete toys i.e. blocks, potato head, swings, etc	Yes	Yes	Yes

 # The Social Skills Checklist — Level 1

Student: _____TIMMY_____	Yes/No 1:1	Yes/No In Group	Yes/No Natural Setting
Module 3 Social Play (continued)			
Sustains imaginative play i.e. restaurant, doctor, trucks, etc.for 15min	NA	NA	NA
w/adult	Yes	Yes	Yes
w/other child	NA	No	No
Shares toys	Yes	Yes	Yes
Trades toys	Yes	Yes	Yes
Stops when peers say "stop"	Yes	Yes	Yes
Ends play appropriately	Yes	Yes	Yes
Cleans up toys when done	Yes	Yes	Yes
Joins in small group free play	NA	No	No
Plays functionally with playground equipment/sustains peer play	NA	No	No
Can sit and play simple game with adults directing	Yes	Yes	Yes
Module 4 Self Awareness			
Ability to tolerate new demands/tasks with support	Yes	Yes	Yes
Ability to delay reinforcement up to 1-2 hours	Yes	Yes	Yes
Accepts interruptions during preferred activity	Yes	Yes	Yes
Asks for help vs. task avoidance	Yes	No	No
Accepts endings/transitions	Yes	Yes	Yes
Accepts 1-2 changes in schedule (flexibility)	Yes	Yes	Yes
Accepts changes in play (flexibility)	Yes	Yes	Yes
Module 5 Conversations			
*Please work with Speech and Language therapists to be sure that all areas of speech and language are addressed appropriately			
States wants/needs (mands) 30+ per day	Yes	Yes	Yes
Labels (tacts) up to 100 minimum	Yes	Yes	Yes
Identifies others by name	Yes	Yes	Yes
Can answer 1-3 social questions i.e. name, age, family names, pet names	Yes	Yes	Yes
Answers others appropriately (no echolalia)	Yes	No	No
Summons/calls others	Yes	Yes	Yes
Answers Yes/No questions appropriately	Yes	No	No
Asks for information: "What is that?" "Where is it?"	Yes	Yes	Yes
Intraverbals of: Fill in blank			
Attributes "What has…"	Yes	Yes	Yes
Categories "Name some…."	Yes	Yes	Yes
Answers "Who" questions	Yes	Yes	Yes
Answers "What" questions	Yes	Yes	Yes

The Social Skills Checklist — Level 1

Student: _____TIMMY_____	Yes/No 1:1	Yes/No In Group	Yes/No Natural Setting
Module 5: Conversations (continued)			
Describes/comments on own actions i.e. "I am (action)"	Yes	Yes	Yes
Asks for attention i.e. "Watch me", "Look at me"	Yes	Yes	Yes
Waits to be called on in a group	Yes	Yes	Yes
Volunteers information on a topic	Yes	No	No
Offers information about school day	Yes	No	No
Module 6: Perspective Taking			
Labels/imitates emotions in pictures	No	No	No
Labels emotions on people, cartoons	Yes	No	No
Labels emotions on self	No	No	No
States what makes child: happy, sad, etc.	Yes	Yes	Yes
Labels body parts on a person hair color, eye color, glasses, etc.	No	No	No
Guesses others imitations of emotions	No	No	No
Looks for/find hidden objects and hides them	Yes	Yes	Yes
Plays charades/imitates another character	Yes	Yes	Yes
Notices & attempts to comfort others	No	No	No
Module 7: Critical Thinking Skills			
Ability to follow schedule/rules	Yes	Yes	Yes
Makes choices out of 3	Yes	Yes	Yes
Understands concept: First, Then	Yes	Yes	Yes
Can sequence pictures up to 4 steps	Yes	Yes	Yes
Can retell 4 pictures in sequence	No	No	No
Can categorize items/themes	Yes	Yes	Yes
Makes basic inferences- "What do you need?" to finish something or make something	No	No	No
Retells events in life/visual aide support	Yes	Yes	Yes
Can find things not present	Yes	Yes	Yes
Can determine "What is wrong" (in pictures)	No	No	No
Can determine "What is same & different" (in pictures)	Yes	Yes	Yes
Can name opposites	Yes	Yes	Yes
Module 8 Advanced Language			
* see level 2			

 # The Social Skills Checklist — Level 1

Student: _____TIMMY_____	Yes/No 1:1	Yes/No In Group	Yes/No Natural Setting
Module 9: Developing Friendships			
Sits next to same peer consistently	NA	No	No
Plays with same peer(s) across several days and several activities	NA	No	No
Shares (snack/toy) with peer	Yes	No	No
Attends birthday party, with peer	No	No	No
Module 10: Community/Home Life			
Home			
Voids in toilet	Yes	Yes	Yes
Undresses when appropriate	Yes	Yes	Yes
Attempts to dress self	Yes	Yes	Yes
Tolerates brushing teeth	Yes	Yes	Yes
Sleeps in own bed	Yes	Yes	Yes
Sits to eat	Yes	Yes	Yes
Remains in home safely	Yes	Yes	Yes
Avoids dangerous situations	Yes	Yes	Yes
Community (some examples)			
Stays with parents in community (up to 20 min)	No	No	No
Go to doctor's appt. successfully	Yes	Yes	Yes
Stays with family in shopping malls/stores	No	No	No
Plays near/with peers in community (bikes, ball, trucks, dolls, etc.)	No	No	No
Holidays:			
Birthday-follows schedule	Yes	Yes	Yes
Waits while others open presents	No	No	No
Halloween- tolerates costume	Yes	Yes	Yes
Other holidays	Yes	Yes	Yes
Sits w/family at meals	Yes	Yes	Yes
Other areas of need:			

Summarizing what skills to teach

After we have completed the Social Skills Checklist, Level 1, we can create a summary of targeted skill areas needed to develop our goals, see below:

Social Skill Targets for Timmy:

Module 1: Joint Attention

O Sitting and attending to new tasks when presented in a small group
O Shifting eyes/body toward peer when listening
O Calling out in unison within a group

Module 2: Greetings

O Walking up to and greeting peer(s) in a group

Module 3: Social Play

O Sustaining imaginative play with peers
O Joining into already established play
O Playing functionally at recess

Module 4: Self Awareness

O Asking for help in novel situations

Module 5: Conversation

O Answering questions asked by peers
O Initiating new conversation topics

Module 6: Perspective Taking

O Imitating emotions
O Labeling other students emotions
O Labeling/noticing advanced body parts on others
  (hair color, clothing color, big or small nose, etc.)

Module 7: Critical Thinking

O Sequencing pictures/retelling story

O Determining "What is wrong/different"
O Determining objects needed to complete an art project

Module 9 Friendships

O Sitting next to peer several times-beginning friendship
O Sharing snack with peers
O Attending party with peers

Module 10 Community/Home life

O Staying with parents in community
O Waiting for others to open presents at holidays

Creating the Program

To review, we have completed a **Social Skills Checklist** and from this, determined a summary of goals for Timmy. These goals will now become a part of Timmy's IEP (Individual Education Plan). His entire team should be familiar with these goals.

Since many of the target skills were not demonstrated in a small group, we'll begin Timmy's program in a small group, with other students with similar needs. We will focus on Timmy's goals and as the group begins to make progress, we'll add peer models, to help generalize skills into a more natural environment.

The following is a program sample for Timmy and the kindergarten social skills group.

Skill work is done during specific activity times, for one hour, two times per week.

*Please see our group format section for teaching social skills later on in chapter 12.

Here is what our proposed program looks like for Timmy:

The Social Skills Program

Child/Group name: _TIMMY/KINDERGARTEN_

SAMPLE STRATEGIES	ACTIVITY	SKILL TARGET	DATA COLLECTION TARGET SKILLS OBSERVED YES/NO	PROMPT LEVEL
Show video of peers greeting other peers	**Arrival**	Greet peers		
Use social story to review peer greeting		Eye contact w/ peer(s)		
Establish reinforcement system for each initiated greeting with good eye contact				
Role play greeting peers		Orient toward		
Sit at a table and present the schedule of the day				
During table time, present worksheet of new information, set up a reward system for completion of this new material, as well as a method for all students to ask for help		Trying new material		
Establish reinforcement for target behaviors to be given at the end of group	**Let's Talk**			
Review eye contact and space- have the student that is talking, put a sticker on his/her face to prompt eye contact		Eye Contact		
Play "show and tell" with a favorite item (trading card, toy) brought to class by each student.		Beginning to initiate topics		
Create conversation by providing cue cards to help students ask questions about item and have the student answer		Ask and Answer questions		
Plan imaginative play scripts-doctor kits, trucks, etc. Show a video of kids playing these games	**Let's Play**	Imaginative Play Joining into play		

The Social Skills Program

Child/Group name: _TIMMY/KINDERGARTEN_

SAMPLE STRATEGIES	ACTIVITY	SKILL TARGET	DATA COLLECTION TARGET SKILLS OBSERVED YES/NO	PROMPT LEVEL
With pictures/written schedules, write-out play scripts	**Let's Play**	Functional recess play		
Role-play and practice greetings		Greeting others		
Practice joining in other's play-show a video of some kids playing-show how a child walks up, and sits down, says "Hi" and starts to play		Acknowledging others Delaying reinforcement Greet others on playground		
Role-play and practice joining play				
Set up reinforcement for demonstration of skill		*Add in, offering help to others		
Work on functional recess play. Set up picture schedules of playing on the equipment, then add in games and asking others to play on this picture schedule				
Spend some time having fun, telling jokes or doing an activity that the children have fun doing and take a picture, print this out and have the students describe that they liked, what they are doing and why it made them happy	**Lets Watch Other**	Perspective taking Beginning emotions States likes/dislikes		
Take other pictures of things they like and have fun with. This is the start of an emotions book.				
Build in conversation: use visual card to help child say to that friend, "I like that", or "That is funny"				
Expand this, taking pictures of things the students don't like, generate lists of likes and dislikes, and the feelings behind this				

As the group progresses, add in other goals not yet addressed into the session

The Social Skills Program - Home Communications

Child/Group name: ___TIMMY___   date _____

1) Today we worked on:

- Talking about our favorite toys, and answering and acknowledging others questions with good eye contact and body positioning.

- Playing imaginary restaurant with 3 other friends

- Greeting others

- Watching funny videos and acknowledging to others around us what we think is funny

2) What you should practice:

- Watching funny/favorite shows with your child, prompting them to tap you or use a visual card that says "That is funny"

- Answering your questions

3) Possible play dates and ideas:

- Timmy seems to have the same interest as Nick. We can help you get together and structure a play date if you want!

4) Suggestions for community goals:

Going to the doctor: Use a social story to let the child know expectations*(comic book pictures work great too). Call ahead and try to pre-arrange with doctor so there is not too long of a wait. Set up a reinforcement system. Start off by delivering a very favorite reinforcer every 30 seconds (or determine baseline starting point) for demonstrating good behavior. Have the doctor do this too! Begin to fade the delivery of reinforcer as necessary. Bring along a book or toy for the child to play with to help maintain desirable behavior.

Please contact us with questions

Data Collection

Data collection is an integral component of a behaviorally based program. It allows us to look at the rate of acquisition of a skill for a student, and to track different interventions or techniques to determine what is the most effective.

The Social Skills Checklist we created and reviewed earlier can provide an abundance of information. By completing the checklist for your children, you can
1. Determine your child's strengths
2. Determine what skills need to be taught
3. Create a baseline of information
4. Create specific goals for intervention and teaching
5. Determine skills the child has learned since the treatment began (post-treatment data)
6. Determine groups based on complimentary needs and strengths

We strongly endorse creativity and inventive teaching styles. However, aside from the children enjoying the activities, there must be evidence (data) to reflect that the activities are more than just fun; they must also be effective at reaching the goals detailed at the outset.

Data can be collected in myriads of ways. The most appropriate method is determined by what the goal is and how it is to be measured (which is made much easier when goals are written in a behavioral format -outlined in the earlier ABA chapter). When teaching a new skill, it is important to record the following:
1. The "SD" or instruction that's given (ex: "touch your nose")
2. Whether your child exhibited the target behavior independently or with assistance
3. If assistance was provided, what prompts were given and by whom
4. Process of generalization: increasing numbers of students, settings, materials and distractions

When measuring social skills progress, data should be collected based on:
1. Frequency — how many times a particular behavior occurred. Ex: how many times your child orients toward the peer talking to him/her.

2. **Rate** — the frequency a target behavior occurs over a predetermined amount of time. Ex: 4 times in 20 minutes.

3. **Duration** — how long your child engages in the target behavior. Ex: appropriate recess play, with a friend, for 15 out of 22 minutes.

4. **Latency** — the measurement of time between the instruction to perform and the occurrence of the targeted behavior. Ex: child responds "Hi" to peer greeting after 5 seconds.

5. **Topography** — description of what the behavior looks like, defined by observable details. Ex: waves his hands in the air, knocks on the door, kicks the desk.

6. **Locus or Place of the Behavior** — where the behavior takes place in the environment, or in reference to the body. Ex: in the classroom, in the cafeteria, pulls own hair, etc.)

Data can be numerical (counting behaviors) or anecdotal (describing events or behaviors with words). A mixture of the two is a good bet, but be certain to write specifics and not generalities. Anyone who reads the data should have a clear picture of the child's abilities and behaviors.

Our Social Skills Solutions Data/Progress Record sheets (see Appendix) are meant to provide a clear and easily manageable way to collect information about your child's progress. Data collection can be a challenge with so many variables effecting social interaction. However, having a specific and individualized data collection system makes it much easier to review progress and plan the future. When recording information on the sheet, be certain that you are recording information that reflects the goal and method of measurement.

Whether you use the strategies listed in this book or design your own interventions and activities, be certain to have a specific goal before you start your session. The goal should reflect exactly what you want your child to accomplish and your strategies should detail the steps necessary to achieve this goal. With this information you will be able to see exactly where your child is struggling and you'll be able to modify the goals for success.

Implementing Social Skills

Teaching 1 to 1

Teaching social skills exclusively in a 1:1 setting has significant drawbacks when it comes to generalization and practical application. However, teaching in a 1:1 setting also has many advantages.

Things to keep in mind about the advantages of 1:1 teaching:

1:1 teaching offers totally individualized instruction, at the pace of your child and can be modified/manipulated easily to accommodate target skills, and important areas such as fluency and decreasing inter-trial interval time (time between trials/tasks).

In a 1:1 setting the opportunity to respond is much more frequent, thereby producing dense response opportunities. Think of the classroom with thirty students and ten spelling words. Even if the teacher asks one student in the class to spell a word from the list, there will only be ten students responding. In a 1:1 setting, one student would have to spell each of the 10 words. Density of response opportunities keeps students on task and attending to the material; thereby creating a greater opportunity to receive feedback and reinforcement.

Working 1:1 with your child may alleviate some of his/her anxiety as he/she may be more aware of expectations and the predictability of the format. It's also easier to respond to your child's potentially increasing anxiety more quickly and appropriately than in a group setting where the anxiety could take the form of inappropriate behaviors (self-stimulatory behavior, self-abusive behavior, outburst, etc.).

In 1:1 teaching, feedback is immediate and specific, allowing your child an opportunity to correct his/her mistake and try again; use this dynamic when teaching a complex skill or to introduce new material. Your child should reach a comfortable level of success before transitioning this skill or material to a group setting.

Teaching in a group

Once a child is ready to generalize skills learned, or is ready to begin learning a new skill within a small group, it can be helpful to start with a small group of children with similar skills and learning profiles. Teach each new skill in a beginning ratio of 1:2 for generalization with other peers, and to benefit all children in the group. Upon mastery of specific skills, introduce other children into the group, including other children from the child's classroom or neighborhood and then expand to outside the classroom.

Here is one sample outline we have used for teaching social skills in a group:
Ideal Group: 3-4 same-aged, similarly skilled children on the spectrum

Needs:
○ Assessment of each child's abilities/needs taken from the Social Skills Checklist, from parents anecdotally and from observations.
○ Assessment of each child's learning style and visual/language ability and review of outside assessments.

Planning:
○ Prioritize social skill goals from the Social Skill Checklist and confirm goals with team.
○ Plan and review curriculum/lesson plans with staff based on the goal areas (using the teaching strategies provided earlier).
○ Outline teaching plan.
○ Prepare visuals, video of some activities for skill being taught (videos of typical peers is preferred).

Actual Group: 55 minutes
○ First 5 minutes: Address goals in Module 2, Greetings, and set the schedule of the group.
○ For 15 minutes: Sit in a circle or around a table to practice listening and attending in a group, Module 1, as well as looking and imitation skills. This is also a good time to ask questions and work on Language/Conversation skills, Module 5.
○ For 25 minutes: "Let's Play" addressing Module 3, Social Play skills. This is a great time to use social skill videos to model desired skills, and then to practice your social play skills, interspersing commenting skills and talking to your friends.
○ For 10 minutes: Work on specialized skills, such as having a snack and practicing conversation skills during this activity, or work on Module 6, Perspective Taking skills, such as reviewing what you played that day, how it made you feel and discussing who is a friend. Taking pictures of play and using these to discuss what happened and how it felt is a great way to discuss feelings as well as for a child to show and re-tell parents what they did.
○ For 5 minutes: wrap-up, help set up play dates, talk about current events, or movies, to keep children in the current mainstream culture. Complete parent homework form.

Using Visuals to Teach

The use of visuals is highly recommended when teaching children with autism. Children with language delays often don't respond well to extensive (verbal) language. Research has told us that this is because there are just too many stimuli happening all at once, and the child is not able to identify the most salient cues.

The use of visuals to support language and more abstract concepts is highly recommended and extremely effective, as it draws on visual scanning and rote memory strengths. Additionally, visual cues help your child understand social rules, can reduce perseveration and maladaptive behaviors and can make transitions more manageable. Visuals can also be used to help facilitate social dynamics, play and increase commenting. As adults, we encounter many naturally occurring and self-imposed visuals throughout our day: watches, traffic signs, to-do lists, etc. We can utilize the same supports for the children we are teaching.

Remember: the use of visuals is only helpful if the visual used has some pre-taught meaning, and reinforcement has been delivered for the appropriate response to the visual! We sometimes see picture schedules that have little or no meaning to the child, because the expectation/correct response has not been taught, the response has not been reinforced, and thus the visual is meaningless to the child.

It should also be noted that we have found that fading a visual cue may be easier than fading a verbal cue. This can be particularly true when dealing with a child's behavioral issues. It can help eliminate a power struggle by relying on a neutral stimulus. The visual cue serves as a reminder for the child, where a verbal prompt is often used as permission. Your child shouldn't be looking to you for "permission"/verbal prompting to engage in social activities or conversations (also known as prompt dependence). Your child should have the tools to be independent!

Here are a few examples of good visual cues to use when teaching skills/motor routines. Remember to use only mastered visual cues, as cues must have meaning to your child.

O Daily picture schedule boards

O Written cues for scheduling the day, where to hang your coat, etc.

O Color coding-red means "Hi", yellow means "Bye"

O Picture Communication Boards: follow PECS protocol

O Behavior reminders: Example: present visual cue of the replacement phrase for the child to access, such as commenting on play instead of talking about trains

O Topic lists: to help a child with conversation

O Task Analysis board: step by step cue for a given task or activity

O Idea Folder: break down unstructured chunks of time into smaller, more manageable components to help structure free time

O Recess schedules and friends charts: to help find someone to play with and activities to participate in

O List acceptable coping strategies for problems and frustration

O Self-monitoring charts: including coping, and managing yourself during difficult times

O Feelings books: to help understand and regulate feelings

O Picture diary: to help a child let his/her parents know what they did at school that day, and build communication

O Homework reminder: outline how to begin work, what steps are necessary, and in which order to complete them

O Behavior Management: for a creative approach to portable behavior management with visuals, refer to the visual appendix section for a reinforcement/token system, communication system, visual rulebook, and daily planner all in one!

Some of our favorite visuals and an explanation on how to implement them are laid out in the appendix. They correspond to many of the teaching strategies we have suggested.

Here are some resources we like to use for visuals:
— Make your own visual cues with digital cameras, or typed words
— Writing with Symbols (Mayer-Johnson) is an excellent software program for printing visuals.
— Refer to Linda Hogdgon's books for a very creative and more complete resource on the use of visuals.
— The website www.do2learn.com has lots of free games and visuals to save and print, as well as visuals to teach emotions, safety and schedules.
— Look for retailers of Pyramid Educational Products for the PECS Communication system in the appendix.

Technology and Video Feedback

The use of video modeling as a teaching tool has been referenced several times in the teaching strategies of this book. We have encountered countless children that don't appear to "pay attention" to the world, yet watch a movie with determination, often memorizing entire scripts to the movie! Why not capitalize on this skill? Whether it is watching movies that have been made for this purpose, taping peers performing correct social skills, or taping your children as a means to giving feedback, it can be a fun activity with an opportunity to learn. In a social skills group that Kelly was running, a video of Kelly and a friend was shown, demonstrating greeting and body positioning. The kids got such a kick out of it, they wanted to watch it at the beginning of every group!

 Capitalize on student's penchant for visually represented material and need for repetition!

Video taping skills may seem time consuming, but for many children this can be a highly effective way to teach. Look for videos such as "Watch Me Learn" made for this purpose. With advances in technology, most people own a video camera or can borrow one. A small but very helpful book on maximizing this technique, by Dr. Liisa Neuman can be found at www.ideasaboutautism.com. This booklet has some great ideas on how you can teach, using video modeling.

○ Make sure the child is able to sit and watch videos and likes to do so.

○ When teaching a skill, systematically tape each component of the skill that you want to teach as though you were teaching the skill in a "how to" video. This may require you to write out every little step so as not to forget any detail.

○ Make sure that the people in the video are fun to watch for the child—try to use people the child generally likes and prefers to be around—try to use peers whenever possible!

○ Make it fun—at the end of each skill you are teaching, try showing a funny picture suddenly, or cut to a funny scene from a favorite show, or someone doing something the child will like—this will be reinforcing for the child and encourage him/her to sit and watch.

○ Have the child watch the video several times before you begin to teach the skill.

You could include as part of the video, an instruction for your child to repeat a word or phrase.

 O Some children may acquire a skill from watching the video just a few times, but some will not. Consider video modeling as a preliminary step in your teaching process and plan several opportunities for repeated exposure.

 O You may need to limit access to some of the child's other favorite videos, or only allow the child to watch them after teaching sessions

As generalization is often difficult or confusing for ASD students, video modeling can be a way to show children how to generalize a skill in a new environment or a setting such as a restaurant, a mall or grocery store. By showing the skills in different settings, a clear expectation is demonstrated, and helps the child visualize exactly what is to be expected. For instance, it can be especially helpful to have a student watch a video of going to his classroom from the bus, or going to the grocery store and waiting in line, without buying candy, at the checkout. The video procedure is this:

Video Modeling:
1. Make it Fun!
2. Keep it positive
3. Encourage kids to comment on themselves and give constructive feedback to others

Have a camera held by a person who will be following the exact same routine the student is expected to follow. Have that person film in the first person- meaning that you never see this person, you only see what he/she is seeing. Include narration and behavior checks ("my hands are down at my side, I am carrying my backpack, I have a quiet voice," etc.) periodically throughout the video. You can add in social elements such as waving to a friend, or greeting people, etc. When viewing this with the student, be certain to point out the most important points of behavior, stating the POSITIVE and what "is" allowed and expected. This means saying "good quiet hands," "nice walking," and "super inside voice" instead of "no touching," "no running," and "don't yell".

Review this several times, and then attempt a return to the previously challenging setting. Remember some key points:

 1. Keep the trip short and successful
 2. Rehearse what will be done and said
 3. Bring a visual or social story to prompt success
 4. Provide lots of feedback and praise for good behavior

5. Try to end the occasion as a SUCCESS

We have also recently made some "homemade" social skills videos. With the help of some great kids, we have made some videos demonstrating many of the skills we wanted to teach, with the kids modeling the expectations. Skills we recently videotaped kids doing included: greetings, asking to join in play, sharing, trading toys, gaining attention of others, eye contact, labeling emotions, and asking why a child was feeling happy/sad/mad/scared, etc. Due to confidentiality and other permission issues, we are unable to share them with you.

This is a video procedure that Janis has used very successfully. In one of her groups, she worked with teens on conversation skills and nonverbal communication. During the group, they practiced the target behaviors/ skills for the day and then made two videos. The first video was the "comedy" or "funny" movie where the student(s) and the teacher make obvious errors in conversation and social interaction for 2-4 minutes. Then, they reviewed the video, to see how many mistakes were made. They record the number of "mistakes" and try to do that many correct things in the "good" movie.

> Great videos for modeling include: Fitting In and Having Fun by T.D. Social Skills, and the Watch Me Learn series. Both videos can be used from start to finish, or by isolating target skills for imitation.

The same procedure for the "good" movie is in effect, as they made sure to use all of the target skills (eye contact, body posture, tone of voice, topic maintenance, etc.) for 3-5 minutes. When they review the "good" movie, the students earn a token or check for each correct skill they identify. Earning all the tokens earns a treat, earning MORE than the set number earns a bonus treat. As an additional bonus, for some older students (relatively speaking!), the making of such an "instructional video" for younger kids was very rewarding and motivating.

Remember, video feedback should be fun and educational not punitive. It is meant to be instructional not embarrassing. We typically ask the students if they would like to make a movie, otherwise, using a digital camera is another option. Making our own video and showing the students ourselves in a "movie" is another way to make it reinforcing and even a preferred instructional tool.

You can also encourage the students to compliment one another and give feedback —POSITIVE ONLY— to one another.

Using Peers to Teach Social Skills

Using peers to teach and reinforce social skills is becoming an increasingly common and effective method for teaching social skills to children with autism. This is important because many times in our assessment of social skills, we find that children with autism are better able to, and prefer to interact and play with adults, and are less able to or show little interest in other children.

There has been a great deal of published literature and research supporting the use of peers to help teach and generalize social skills. One website that lists a great deal of information about the topic, as well as a very comprehensive research review is www.feat.org/autism/social_skills.htm. On this website there are several reviews of studies that support the use of using peers to help generalize and increase the opportunities of social interactions with children with autism. A common thread in the literature recommends initial training of the peers and peer buddies prior to beginning work with the child with autism.

Dr. Bridget Taylor has done a significant amount of research and writing on the topic of teaching children with autism to interact with peers. In a chapter in the book Making a Difference, she notes that teaching children with autism to learn from and interact with peers can be challenging. As a result, effective instruction in peer interaction skills requires thoughtful and specific planning. From her research review, Dr. Taylor makes several important conclusions:

○ Pre-teaching is necessary for the peers.

○ Specific reinforcement procedures are required to encourage and ensure that interactions occur.

○ Additional strategies may be needed to help maintain interactions and promote. generalization. In other words, peer training may not be enough— paired with reinforcement, a carefully structured environment is also required.

○ Although peers may be taught to initiate with the child with autism, the child with autism may not always engage or respond. Equal emphasis on teaching initiation to the child with autism will help reinforce the peer to keep going.

Choosing peers:

Choosing a peer is one of the most important choices one can make in structured peer sessions. Some suggested criteria for choosing peers:

○ It is helpful if the child is slightly older, or slightly more mature.

○ It is helpful to have a child that will reliably respond to directions.

○ It is helpful to have a child that has age-appropriate language and social skills.

○ It is helpful to have a child that is interested in helping others; although there is sometimes a tendency for children to take on a "mothering" role to the child with autism, it is best to address this during preliminary peer training and give specific instructions and guidelines. Keep in mind that other children may be taking their cues of how to interact from this child. Create the appropriate dynamics from the beginning. Do not try to "mother" and do too much for the child.

○ It is helpful to pair up same gender whenever possible, to have a true reflection of age and gender appropriate skills.

○ It is helpful to have a child that will be available for all of your teaching sessions.

When you find peers like this, you are ready!

Teaching peers:

Many peers/children feel that they benefit a great deal from working with other children with autism. Comments from some peer buddy students reflect their feelings:

"I like helping the kids because they are just like us"

"I like working with people like May because you learn more and get to help others. You could teach others how to use wheelchairs and stuff like that"

"I like helping Tom because you learn more about people who need help"

"It's cool to play the games with them like kickball and help"

"I like the snacks and playing basketball; Mike is good at it"

Buddy programs are popping up in many school systems, with children rewarded for their time spent as buddies. Some very good work is happening with these programs, but some are faltering due to lack of organization and training for the peer buddies.

When training your peers, it is important to think about what specific information about the child with autism is to be shared with the peers. It is suggested that information be shared on an individual basis and left up to the parents and the child's educational team.

Some very talented teachers Kelly has worked with in California (Erin Davenport-Spinello, Misty Amon and Cindy Terhune) have done some terrific training with buddies, teaching the buddies to "walk in the shoes" of a child with autism. These teachers put together visual handouts explaining autism. They spent time showing students what it was like to have trouble with fine motor skills by having the buddies do things with thick gloves on. They have the buddies take in a lot of information from the teacher that is presented half in English and half in a foreign language to see what it is like to have language processing difficulties. The buddies in this program were very committed buddies!

Training peers should happen several times during your peer program. Initial training should be done prior to using your peers. After the initial training, providing feedback, training and support is recommended. Read the book Trevor Trevor, by Diane Twachtman-Cullen. It's great!

Try using the following training Do's and Don't with your peers. It may help to draw pictures of the skills or act out the scenarios with your peers, for a greater impact.

HELPFUL HINTS FOR A PEER BUDDY!
Do's:
- O <u>Do get the child's attention</u> first, and then give directions.
- O <u>Do respond</u> to what the child is doing. Play with the toys the child likes to play with.
- O <u>Do the same thing</u> the child is doing with a toy.
- O When the child is playing with you, <u>Do keep on playing.</u>
- O <u>Do show him/her what to do</u> by playing with another peer. Let the child watch you and do what you are doing.
- O <u>Do tell the child when they are doing a good job</u>. Compliment and praise the child.
- O <u>Do give the child time to respond</u>. If you want the child to throw a ball to you, hold your hand out and wait.
- O <u>Do change activities</u> if the child loses interest.
- O <u>Do start playing close to the child</u> and then move away slowly so the child knows what to do.

Don't:
- O Don't try to compete with one another. <u>Take turns</u> to come up with ideas.
- O Don't keep saying his/her name over and over again. Instead, try and show him the toy or hold your hand out to <u>gain attention</u>.

Peer Buddy Programming:

Once you have your peer buddies trained, you can plan your social skills teaching right from the assessments and teaching strategies outlined in this book.

Use the Social Skills Checklists to determine what functional social skills need to be a priority for the child.

Once you have determined the skills you will be teaching, draw from the teaching strategies and devise a systematic teaching process.

Use your buddies to promote and teach. Make sure and take data on your prompting levels, independent responses, as well as skill generalization, mixing up buddies or increasing the size and number of students in the group.

Use necessary visual supports to help support the child. Some examples of visuals to use can be found in the appendix section of this manual.

Here is a sample programming curriculum:

Monthly Social Skills Teaching — Sample curriculum ideas

MONTH	SKILLS
September/October	Greeting peers • "Hi" • "Hi name"

	Joint Attention
	    • Look/orient to person
	    • Build together

	Recess/Play
	    • Teach functional recess play
	    • Use visual boards-set up recess stations

November	Greetings
	    • Expand to greet classmates and
	    • Buddies by name

	Joint Attention
	    • Look at person for greeting
	    • Joint task: pass/kick ball back and forth min. 5 times

	Beginning Conversation
	    • Use visual: Find friend and
	    • Say "Let's Play"

	Recess/Play • With buddy, fade visual as appropriate

December	Greetings
	    • Students initiate greeting
	    • Expand: "Hi, What's up?"

	Joint Attention • Begin board-game play

	Beginning Conversation
	    • Respond to questions
	    • Group tasks: compare likes/dislikes

A classroom "Buddy Center" can be another great way to promote the buddy idea and encourage kids to learn more about the "program" on their own time. The center should be a very positive place with ideas and encouragement for the program.

Some ideas for a Buddy Center:
- A colorful box labeled "My favorite things to do that I would like to share with or teach a friend". These activities can be a great way for your child to find out what toys other kids want to share and what activities they like to do.
- "Find Out About a Friend" worksheet pages that list questions that students can ask one another to find out about their classmates and discover common interests and special talents. (See "Appendix")
- "Everyone has things they are good at". Activity: create a list (with words, or pictures of) each child's strengths. Look at common patterns to see who has the same strengths.
- "We have things in common". Activity: have the students make a list of things they like and things they don't like. They can cut out pictures from magazines, draw, or write the words. Display or have a group discussion about what things everyone has in common.
- "Please help me". Teach children to ask for help and work together. Activity: with children in pairs, have one child wear mittens and ask him/her to perform a difficult task, like peeling off a sticker and placing it on their shirt or bulletin board. Teach the children wearing mittens to ask their partner for help, have the team complete the task.
- We all "work together" to create one big picture. Activity: like a giant puzzle, each child gets a shape and each shape is added to build one big picture, such as a big train or mural.
- Set up a video station, showing videos of children participating in target social skills (we are involved in research in this area right now).
- Celebrate favorite buddy moments and good deeds by creating small certificates that can be posted with accompanying photographs on a bulletin board.
- "Buddy Marble Jar": when good buddy interactions are noticed, a marble is placed in the buddy jar, when the jar is full the class receives a special treat. The treat should be chosen by the class as motivation. This approach targets collective efforts and teamwork. It may be necessary to start off with a small jar, and small treat, to provide short-term reinforcement and establish the concept.
- Create an ongoing Buddy Scrapbook: a large scrapbook that students can contribute to with pictures, notes, cards, photos, drawings, etc. to be kept as a classroom memento.

O Have a disposable camera to take "Buddy Shots" and display them on your bulletin board. You can also use these pictures to help the students make the friend charts mentioned earlier.

O Keep plenty of worksheets available with activities (mastered by the child with autism) to do during free time and recess.

O Post your buddy "Do's and Don'ts Checklist" (provided earlier in this manual) as a reminder.

O Review weekly or monthly buddy target skill(s) and make sure the classroom support team knows what skills they are working on.

**See "appendices" for corresponding worksheets for buddy centers*

Our Friend Chart is an idea we used to help the students learn how to initiate play and invite a friend to play in a variety of activities. It also encourages the student to choose different peers.

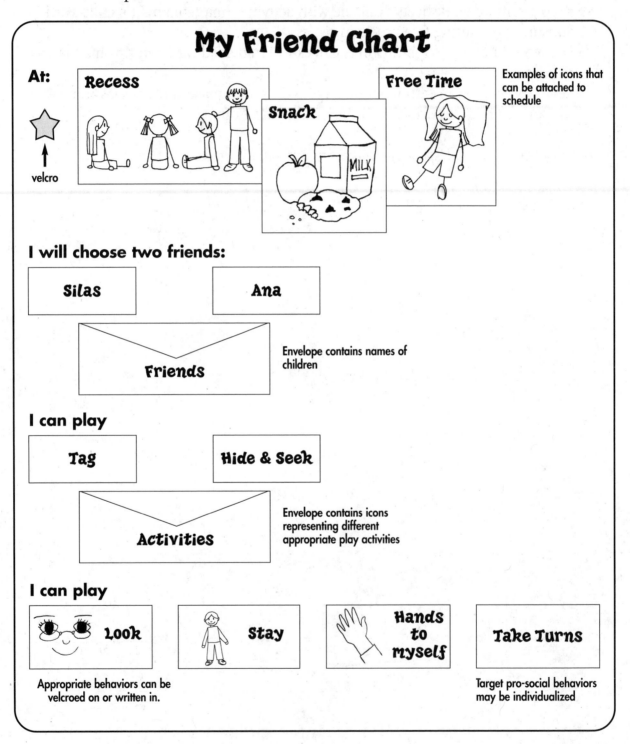

My Friend Chart

At:

Recess

Snack

Free Time

Examples of icons that can be attached to schedule

velcro

I will choose two friends:

Silas   Ana

Friends

Envelope contains names of children

I can play

Tag   Hide & Seek

Activities

Envelope contains icons representing different appropriate play activities

I can play

Look   Stay   Hands to myself   Take Turns

Appropriate behaviors can be velcroed on or written in.

Target pro-social behaviors may be individualized

Bulletin Boards are a great way to punctuate a concept and keep the topic current in the classroom. Students can access the board at any time and with the right support from the teacher, it can be an opportunity for conversation, reference, reinforcement and encouragement for the whole class! The bulletin boards can include pictures of the students, magazine cut outs, drawings and photos from play dates. This concept can easily be done at home and displayed on the refrigerator. It's also good to have a classroom disposable camera to take pictures of peers and post new pictures every few weeks! If you can find "double prints free" offers, students can be encouraged to take these pictures home and share them with their families, thereby providing an opportunity for generalization of many skills, including storytelling and initiating conversation. Please send us your photographs and ideas, we will post them on our website!

Topics for bulletin boards can include:

Being a Friend
O Help your friend
O Ask your friend to play
O Sit with your friend at lunch
O Play with your friend at recess
O Smile at your friend
O Share toys with your friend
Include pictures of the friends!

Compromise
O Take turns
O Share
O Ask a grown up for help
O Listen to your friends
O Talk it over
O Your way + My Way + Compromise = Our Way

Being Flexible
(verbal cues and coping strategies)
O Change is okay
O Next time is a good time
O It's something new!

Conversation/Find Out About Us
O Choose the question –
    ex. What is your favorite game?
    Color? Do you have any pets?
O Post pictures of the student's and the answers. Create student profiles.

Being a Good Sport
O It's okay to lose
O "That was fun, let's do it again!"
O "You can choose the next game"
O "Oops! I'll try again next time"
O "Good game"

Friendly words to say
O "Hello!"
O "I like your drawing!"
O "That's really cool!"
O "That looks great!"
O "You did a great job!"
O "Can I help you with that?"
O "Can I play, too?"
O "See you later!"

Social Skills and Inclusion

Parents of children with autism often say that they simply want their child to be liked, and to have a friend or two. This statement always seems like a small and reasonable request, after all, there is a lot to like about these children! Many times schools are faced with this request and parents are angry when friendships are not forged at school—a place that is filled with potential friends!

For the child with autism, unfortunately, making friends is not as easy as it would seem. With typically developing children, the ability to make friends tends to happen in a naturally occurring developmental process through observation of others, play, and natural curiosity—a process that relies heavily on the skills that are lacking in the diagnosis of autism.

After working with some very insightful and savvy children with autism, we have come to understand that the skill of social interest and making friends can be and needs to be taught. Unfortunately, some parents and teachers may immediately think that this means their child needs Inclusion. We have a few additional thoughts to consider in this process toward developing friendships and social skills.

 For the purposes of our book and to have a working definition for this chapter, let's define social inclusion as: *the ability to accept an invitation to participate in an activity with peers; and to be able to appropriately engage in the activity, and reciprocate the invitation.*

This definition will help us more concretely task analyze social opportunities and teach the prerequisite skills such as greetings, commenting, imitation, reciprocity in verbal and non-verbal interactions, play-skills, and more.

The challenge of merging the academic component of your child's education, along with the social opportunities that occur in a classroom environment becomes a critical balancing act in your child's overall programming. Once again, we refer to the diagnostic criteria to prioritize our expectations for the student:

    O Language   O Behavior
    O Cognitive/Academic   O Social

Presenting challenging demands in all four areas simultaneously may be overwhelming for your child and often invites an increase in maladaptive behavior, self-stimulatory behavior and non-compliance.

Frequently, students with autism have come from highly specialized teaching programs. In order to have continued success, the student needs to be taught the skill of how to acquire new information at a comparable rate of success. Simply placing the student in an inclusion setting just because he/she has met some prerequisite criteria does not mean that he/she will be successful acquiring new information and learning new skills in that setting. Assuming and expecting the student to acquire new skills in a novel situation, via unfamiliar or less specialized delivery of instruction (i.e. lecture or large group formats) is NOT an appropriate expectation.

We are suggesting an additional criterion for inclusion. The student must already possess the skills to acquire new information in the generalized format and large group instruction or be able to work towards learning skills used in inclusion settings (such as lecture, large group or independent work).

It is unrealistic to expect an aide to compensate for the lack of student skills. The student should be able to handle transitions with few problems, since they may be leaving the classroom frequently for therapies and 1:1 work with specialists, while simultaneously learning new information in this more generalized way.

Some students are placed in inclusive settings to address generalization. When done systematically and data-driven, this can be effective. Some students are placed in inclusive settings to target social skills. However, a word of caution, based on the student's abilities and current skills, be sure to prioritize expectations for the student in each setting/activity throughout the day. Evaluate the social demands during time scheduled for the presentation of new academic skills; maintain an appropriate level of response criteria based on the setting and the student's ability to work effectively in that setting within each of the four areas mentioned above.

In her chapter in the book Making a Difference, Dr. Bridget Taylor comments about the time allocated for peer social skill instruction that we fully support. Dr. Taylor notes that if a child, just beginning their programming, engages in high rates of stereotypical and disruptive responses, does not reliably imitate others, and has little functional speech, then programming time is better spent addressing those specific skills [and other areas as identified in skill assessments] in a specialized setting.

Dr. Bridget Taylor, Ms. Linda Meyer and Ms. Susan Johnson, are three clinicians who have researched supported inclusion extensively and wrote a chapter in Behavioral Intervention for Young Children with Autism. In this chapter, the researchers state that full inclusion should be subjected to empirical verifications and that data become the basis for making decisions about which children with autism should be integrated full-time.

They have listed important empirical criteria that they feel is fundamental when deciding about supported inclusion, criteria that we believe should be used by all practitioners, schools, and parents when making decisions about supported inclusion. These include, but are not limited to:
  o Having good language skills, both expressively and receptively
  o Having some beginning social skills, including being able to wait, taking turns and participating in circle activities
  o Learning in both 1:1 and small group instruction
  o Exhibiting disruptive behaviors at near-zero
  o Having some control over stereotypic behaviors
  o Being near grade level academically

Proximity to typical children is not enough, and will not accomplish the behavior, social, and academic goals set forth. Exposure to typical children is not the variable here; inclusion requires facilitated interactions and carefully designed and implemented social programs. When looking at the criteria that Dr. Taylor outlines, and looking at the children that are currently placed in included settings, we begin to see a significant discrepancy between their skill levels and the appropriate skills needed for their placement. Unfortunately there does not exist a myriad of appropriate educational settings, it is up to us as educators to use the research to create and place children in the best and most appropriate educational environment based on their individual needs. We propose a teaching setting that is data-driven.

Think of inclusion as a learning continuum:

When it has been decided by the team that inclusion is appropriate, then a placement and program needs to be determined. However, a successful inclusion experience is much more than a serendipitous match of "appropriate timing", based on age and

Child acquires new skills in a 1:1 situation	Child acquires new skills in a 2:1 or small group	Child acquires new skills in a classroom/large group
Recommend Autism specific Classroom & ABA 1:1 programming	**Recommend** Structured class Small group Instruction	**Recommend** Inclusion Initial aide support Plan to fade aide support
Address 1:1 Social Goals	**Address** small group learning social skills	**Address** social skills

program availability. We believe that for successful inclusion, there are many crucial components that dovetail with one another. No link can be weak or partial, the inclusion "program" is a team effort, and a team success, on behalf of the student with autism. Outlined below are mainstays for a successful inclusion program.

Successful inclusion relies on careful consideration of the following—before placement. (Myles, et. al, 1993)

1. Carefully planned and orchestrated integration programs with specific goals, target skills, and criteria for success. Programming includes making use of social skill programs, direct instruction for social skills, and planned opportunities for generalization. Prompting strategies should maximize student success and independence with peers, effectively.

2. Facilitated integration and inclusion through attitude-modification programs and procedures. This means awareness and sensitivity programs for student and staff in the inclusion setting.

3. Class-size — ideally the inclusion class should have a reduced number of students for the following reasons:
a. To maximize opportunity for individualized instruction
b. To promote greater likelihood of creative lesson planning and instructional methodologies
c. To minimize behavior problems

d. To more precisely match students for integration opportunities

If you and your child have come this far and the program meets the criteria, then your child is "ready" for inclusion. For inclusion to be successful, it is recommended that an on-site facilitator be provided by the school, as a full time position. This person would insure consistency across the day for the student, facilitate communication with all teachers and professionals, and maintain a cohesive daily structure for the student (insuring there is generalization and maintenance of skills). We suggest that this is a master's level position, requiring experience in teaching students with autism, and have successful experience working in inclusive settings with children with special needs.

Some schools are adopting this model by hiring "Autism Specialists" or "Inclusion Coordinators" that are highly trained individuals in the field of behavior modification, special education, and/or autism. It's also important to note that in addition to education, this person needs to communicate effectively, recognize when his/her staff is in need of support, reinforcement or reward and be able to recognize possible problems in an effort to avoid catastrophe for either staff or student.

The role of the teacher is to teach. The role of the aide is to follow the lead of the classroom teacher, and support the student, with as least restrictive prompts as necessary for success, and to teach toward learning directly from the teacher. The Inclusion Coordinator is then able to review the needs of the child, making sure that supports and curriculum are modified and in place to reach this optimal placement.

We would like to add that, the National Research Council, in their text, Educating Children with Autism, 2001, states that "for a child with an autistic spectrum disorder to be included in mainstream settings, the child must be able to manage social experiences. This requires careful consideration on the part of the school staff".

Of equal importance, initial and ongoing staff training should be conducted by a behavior specialist, ideally, someone who is also very familiar with the child. The person training the staff should implement accountability measures with the teachers and staff to insure consistency and maximum support.

It's been our opinion that children and their programs benefit most from regular and efficient communication among team members. By regular, we mean consistently scheduled contact meetings at appropriate intervals (daily, twice weekly, weekly...depending on the frequency of contact between the specialist and the student). By efficient, we mean communication should be specific and related to target goals and issues.

Communication and data collection should streamline information and be easy to record, easy to ascertain, and easy to evaluate. This type of efficiency in communication helps to maintain focus and allows for review of progress. This is not the forum for blame or isolation. It is the opportunity to work collaboratively, to support one another, focusing on the child's success and solution driven strategies.

In addition to training and reference, here are some other important tips to ensure the success of the educational support team of the child with autism. They need:
1. Clearly defined job descriptions and responsibilities for each team member
2. Clearly defined methods of feedback and data collection
3. Accessible supervision and support
4. Clearly defined hierarchy of supervision and decision making

Remember the priorities we spoke of earlier (behavior, language, social and academics)? Well, let's talk about ways to accommodate students after those priorities have been established. Many times the student with autism will need to work on activities or assignments in a different way than his peers. That is okay, remember, SUCCESS and INDEPENDENCE are vital. If you find that the modifications are too numerous and extensive, you may want to have a team meeting to review the goals and the placement. Aside from that, curriculum and social accommodations are daily challenges, constantly weighing in on precisely appropriate response criterion, while keeping your child challenged and part of the classroom. Outlined below are some examples of curriculum and participation adaptation strategies:
1. **Size:** Adapt the number of items that the learner is expected to learn or to complete.
2. **Time:** Adapt the time allotted and allowed for learning, task completion or testing.
3. **Level of Support:** Increase the amount of personal assistance with a specific learner (teacher, staff, tutor or peer).
4. **Input:** Adapt the way instruction is delivered to the learner (use different visual aides, plan concrete examples, provide hands—on activities, place students in cooperative groups).
5. **Difficulty:** Adapt the skill level, problem type or the rules on how the learner may approach the work (allow the use of a calculator, simplify directions, change rules to accommodate learner's needs).
6. **Output:** Adapt how a student can respond to instruction (allow verbal rather than

written responses, use a communication book, allow students to demonstrate knowledge with hands on materials).

7. **Participation:** Adapt the extent to which a learner is actively involved in the task (having the student hold lesson stimuli while other students comment on them).

8. **Alternate:** Adapt the goals or outcome expectations while using the same materials as the regular education students.

9. **Substitute Curriculum:** provide different instruction and materials to meet a student's individual goals**.

**From: *Adapting Curriculum and Instruction in Inclusive Classrooms: A Teacher's Desk Reference by Deschenes, C., Ebeling, D., and Sprague, J. 1994*

Remember:
When we place a child in an inclusive setting, we are presupposing that the child is currently able to acquire novel information and skills in this type of setting and exhibits minimal to zero inappropriate or disruptive behaviors.

Until the child with autism has the necessary skill set to play and interact with other children, the child will most likely not fully benefit from their inclusion experience. However, with the necessary skill set taught, using peers and inclusion can be very successful. A helpful book in the inclusion series by Sheila Wagner, M.A., Inclusion Programming for Middle School Students with Autism/Asperger's Syndrome, (2002) can be a very practical book to review. This book series looks at the typical profile of students and writes about the split in skills that can occur in academics, adaptive behaviors and social skills.

Ways to ensure successful social/academic opportunities include the following behavioral strategies:

1. **The use of backward chaining** — introducing a student to the end of an activity and having them complete it successfully with peers, and then systematically increasing the amount of time the student participates, until the student is beginning and ending the activity with his peers.

2. **Gradual exposure** — "trying out" a new activity or setting during times when the student is most likely to be successful, systematically increasing time in the activity or setting.

3. **Increased rate/frequency of feedback to student** — while a student may be able to handle delayed reinforcement and less frequent feedback in a 1:1 setting, when in an inclusion program (especially initially) it may be helpful to provide the student with increased frequency of feedback, through tokens, praise, non-verbal

cues, and proximity (standing closer or farther away).

4. **Reinforce success**, but REALLY reinforce success with INDEPENDENCE— for some students, they are happy just to have the task or activity completed, and are fine with prompts and cues from an aide or teacher. Always promote independence, and when in the company of peers, be certain to use the least restrictive (most socially innocuous) prompt available.

5. **Teach the student to look at his peers** for information about an assignment or what to do, use peers as a reference, not requiring the teacher to repeat an instruction. (This is a crucial life skill, too!)

If your child is not yet ready for inclusion, it is important to work toward this, by systematically teaching skills and generalizing these skills to larger group settings, with variances in peers, adults, and materials. In a social setting, there are many opportunities throughout a school day to practice.

Free play: Free play is not generally successful for a child with autism that does not have an extensive play repertoire. Developing age appropriate play skills and flexibility is key; suggestions for teaching and enhancing these skills were described in an earlier section of this manual. One extremely successful way to promote social play during free play and recess is to set up "play stations", and pair the child with a peer buddy to move from station to station. Begin by: setting up age-appropriate play stations/areas such as 1) manipulative/puzzle station 2) cooperative building (either with blocks, or on the computer, etc.) 3) dramatic play-pretend play taught by using scripts as needed to teach the dramatic play area or more advanced play such as putting on plays 4) sensory/fun trading/sharing station 5) board game stations. Have a paraprofessional or support staff at several of the stations (or ones that seem to be a bit more challenging and needing increased support or supervision) to facilitate in each play area. Pair the child with autism with a peer buddy to move from station to station. Use a timer to signal the beginning and ending of each play interval. Using visuals outlining appropriate language, behavior and play topics can also significantly increase independence and appropriate play skills. Also helpful may be pre-teaching with the materials in a smaller setting, using the same stimuli and visual cues.

Gym class: This can be a great way to generalize joint attention skills. Gym class is often comprised mostly of motor-tasks and joint attention, with little language. In your play teaching, as you generalize play skills, move towards common gym class games and then generalize into the gym class.

Lunch/Snack: Even though we teach children not to talk with their mouths full, lunch is often a good time to teach some conversation. Adults and kids constantly talk about food—what we have to eat, what we don't like to eat, what we ate earlier that day....on and on. This is great to teach the child with autism to do too. This will probably have to be prompted. Visual scripts for the child, teach how to ask others about what they have for lunch, and then comment on their lunch. They can be slipped right into a lunch box, and used over and over again. Finding a peer that has something for lunch that the child with autism has will really help move the process along! Language such as "I have", "I like__", "I don't like__", "What do you have", "What do you like?" are great conversation starters. Also, be sure to listen in on conversations and find out what other kinds of topics are being discussed (movies, toys, vacations, etc.) Try having the child put a small favorite item in their lunch bag/box, role-play and use visual scripts to teach the child how to show it and describe it to their friends.

Recess: Many times the child with autism can be seen standing on the periphery of the playground, or standing near a toy or playground equipment, not playing appropriately. We like to set-up recess for younger children much the same as the play stations noted above. Visual schedules (written or pictures) are very helpful in teaching a child to navigate the recess area. Pairing a peer or buddy up to complete the schedule is a great way to increase social interactions. A schedule may have pictures that direct a child to: climb and slide; climb and slide, say "Hi" to a friend; swing, get drink, go to class. Or, if the child can read, use a written schedule that says: Find one friend. Play that friend's game. Choose a different friend, ask them to play your game. Play for five minutes.

** It is important to note that some initial teaching and reinforcement around following the schedule may be needed, but pairing the child up with the buddy will also help. Use a recess chart. See the appendix for some sample visuals.

Peer/Buddy time: Structured social opportunities such as "buddy time" will also benefit the child with autism. Pre-teaching your peers how to be a buddy, along with outlining the specific skills to teach the child with autism, and using age appropriate toys and games are three essential ingredients for social success with peers. Board or card games, sharing a computer to teach turn-taking, waiting, and commenting can be very beneficial. Help your child learn his/her friend's names by using a picture chart of buddies and classmates. Have the peer buddy play with your child and teach him/her new things. Many times a child will do things for other children that they would never do for adults! Playing with and learning from other children is the goal! See chapter 12 on using peers to teach social skills.

Art class and Music class: Art and Music classes can also be great when structured and paired with a peer! These may be low-demand for your child, and therefore great opportunities to pair with a friend. (or may be too much for a child with sensory issues— consider this!). Provide your child with any/all necessary visuals (picture or written word schedule, list of rules, etc.) to make the situation as positive as possible. Many times it is easier for the student with autism to follow along modeling a peer, then it is to have to listen to large group instruction.

Additional strategies: Make a book about your child's friends and peers in the class-room. Create an interview sheet that asks questions such as, "Do you have a pet?" "What do you do after school?" "What is your favorite toy?" "What is your favorite color?" Have your child interview his/her peers, and then create a reference book about his/her friends. This will help later on in teaching what to talk about with certain friends based on what they like. It can also be used to help structure conversation, and can be especially helpful as a classroom project in the beginning of the school year, when kids are just getting to know one another.

Circle time: Large group instruction is frequently an enormous challenge for the child with autism. Frequent feedback and a tangible or concrete reinforcement system (tokens) and visual support to supplement the teaching is necessary (visual supports can also serve to increase non-verbal participation by having the child with autism hold, place, move or act-out lesson related material). Additionally, it may be helpful to have a peer or buddy sit next to the child with autism and help the child by directing him with visuals, modeling appropriate behavior such as imitation to song, and providing social or other means of reinforcement. Visually represented behavior and language expectations can also be extremely helpful to the student, and reduces intrusive verbal prompting and cueing during the teacher's lesson.

The Role of Parents

According to the text, Educating Children with Autism, 2001, by the National Research Council, "while many families cope well with the demands [of having a child with autism], the education of a child with autism can be a source of considerable stress...(e.g. Bristol et all, 1988; Harris, 1994)" .

The text goes on to say, "because of the nature of autism, young children with the disorder need a consistent and supportive environment to make optimal educational progress".

Parents can learn techniques for teaching their children adaptive skills and management behaviors that:
- make home life more manageable
- are not counter-indicative to other skills being taught
- facilitate generalization of skills taught elsewhere.

For many parents, this role is sometimes overwhelming given that social skills training in particular tends to happen in the school environment or in a specialized program. Therefore it is vital that the family play an instrumental role in their child's educational plan. We addressed some of this in Module 10. Generalization, as we know, is not spontaneous for children with autism and skill transfer can be a challenge. Here are a few tips for parents to help their children in the process.

1. Establish a relationship with the team and with individual service providers and stay informed. Communication is paramount and it needs to be reciprocal. You need to let the staff know when there are issues, and they, in turn, should keep you informed as to how and when the issues will be addressed and consequently, resolved.

However you decide to communicate, please do so with functional, data-based information. Spend time writing about both strengths and areas of need, as well as keeping all team members "on the same page" about what interventions and tools are being used with your child. It is not fair, nor effective, for your child to have different people doing different intervention strategies. We cannot say enough about the importance of team communication. When we see families and schools not working together as a team, we generally see the child with autism not achieving as favorably as possible.

2. Establish consistency in your expectations for your child, across settings and people. This is the biggest challenge, but well worth the efforts. If you're communicating with the staff, you will know about new skill acquisitions and can maintain high expectations at home. This will reduce behavior problems and help your child to practice his skills for generalization and mastery. Everyone in the household should have the same expectations, not allowing your child to avoid unpleasant or difficult tasks.

3. Make use of rehearsal strategies, visuals, and modeling. Provide clear expectations and lots of positive feedback and reinforcement. All of these suggestions have been outlined throughout this book and will be helpful in the home environment. Using the same or similar visuals will go along way to help with consistency and therefore behavior change.

4. Play dates with peers are a great way to increase social opportunities. Having a peer come over to play in a setting where the toys are familiar, the rules are familiar, and routines have been long established, facilitates success. The only added variable that your child will need to negotiate is the peer. Choose peers wisely. In Chapter 12 we provided some helpful information regarding the use of peers. If peers are not readily available, siblings and cousins can also play! Initially play dates should be kept short and successful. Long afternoon play dates are best kept for older students who have a large repertoire of play/leisure skills and self-management skills.

5. Get to know the parents of the children in your neighborhood and in your child's class. A little networking will be helpful in planning frequent play dates and finding a good friend for your child.

As a parent, it may be up to you to bridge the gap from a peer at school to a "friend with something in common" through play dates. As a parent, you are a good resource, you will have longer blocks of time that are not always afforded in the classroom setting to address social play. It is often unreasonable to expect that your child will naturally "generalize" any skills they have learned to the home or neighborhood setting. Often times you may need to start over in this setting—the good news is skill acquisition should go faster if your child has learned what to do in other settings.

The use of visuals to set up expectations, as well as reinforcement for a "job well done", along with the other strategies we have provided, will equip you with the skills to facilitate. As a parent, you have access to rewards that are not allowed at school, such as video game time or computer time, that will be more powerful to motivate and shape your child's skills.

Quick Tips for Teachers and Paraprofessionals

Despite the title of this chapter, parents should keep reading this chapter. Paraprofessionals may become an important person in your child's life and it is often helpful if everyone understands the training needs and expectations of paraprofessionals, as it can be a very demanding and technical job. As parents, you will want to know this information to ensure that your child receives the best education possible.

Appropriate training for all teachers and support staff is essential for ensuring the success of your child with autism. There are many good trainers and books on the subject. A good resource is How to be a ParaPro, A Comprehensive Training Manual for Paraprofessionals, by Dianne Twachtman-Cullen, Ph.D. This manual is easy to read and describes a great deal of important information about autism and how to understand and support your child.

We believe a behavior specialist should conduct training of paraprofessionals. Additional training by someone very familiar with the child can also be very helpful. Training for paraprofessionals should include the following points:

1. Thorough review of the diagnosis of autism
    a. Diagnostic criteria
    b. Learning styles
2. Review of child's previous educational settings
    a. Likes/dislikes
    b. What was previously successful/unsuccessful
    c. Learning styles
    d. Behaviors
    e. Current skill levels
3. ABA and Behavioral Intervention
    a. Prompting hierarchies and strategies
    b. Data collection
    c. Presenting new information to a student

4. Additional teaching strategies
   a. How to best use peers for promoting social interaction
   b. The use of visual strategies

This list is not comprehensive by any means, but it serves as a foundation for tutor/paraprofessional training.

In addition to training and reference manuals, here are some other important tips for the support team of children with autism:

Paraprofessional Checklist

O Know your goal in each situation. Don't react/prompt until you know what you want your planned outcome to be. React to meet that outcome.

O Stay within view of the student at all times, fade the distance as appropriate, but always be close enough to prompt both the teacher to the student and the student to the teacher when necessary to keep the student successful.

O Think about prompting—don't do too much and "mother" the child and don't miss an opportunity for the child to achieve success.

O Fade to non-verbal prompts (gestures, points, written cues) as quickly as possible, so that your presence does not interrupt the student's active learning process. Do use visuals and gestures: use picture/written lists and charts. Talking too much to a child with language processing difficulties is not helpful. Teaching the child to rely on him/herself and available resources will have many reinforcing applications.

O Be prepared!! Anticipate difficult areas, be prepared to work proactively.

O Reinforce, Praise, Reinforce!!

O Make expectations clear, with clear points. Don't leave the child to guess what you want, or guess when he/she is finished.

O Allow the child to work through difficulties, to problem solve. Do not provide the answer immediately. Use this as an opportunity to try and teach the student problem solving skills.

O Teach independence as much as possible throughout the day, especially with things such as organizing papers, folders, desk supplies, lunch, library, etc.

O Prompt the child to follow all classroom rules, just like typical peers.

O Prompt the child to raise his/her hand appropriately to seek clarification/ask/answer/volunteer information-don't do it for them.

O Only one person at a time should be giving directions to the child—follow the example set by the classroom teacher and consultant.

O Fill out communication books or data sheets accurately and thoroughly—these books will be guiding the program of the child. Nothing should be assumed and everything should be documented. Communication is essential if everyone is to be aware of what's going on with the child.

O Expect/demand the training and support you need.

APPENDICES

School/Home Visual Strategies

Visual Idea: My Idea Folder

This folder was created to provide a strategy for addressing executive functioning challenges, in other words "I'm bored!" or "I don't know what to do!" dilemmas. Creating and using activity schedules are fabulous tools and much has been written about their implementation. This idea is linked to those schedules, but for higher functioning students.

The idea is that there are several small cards in each of the three categories, Inside, Outside and Responsibilities. Each card has one activity written on it.

Inside cards may include: play a board game, make a snack, listen to music, do homework, call a friend on the phone, watch 30 minutes of TV, complete a puzzle, read a book with Dad, etc.

Outside activities may include: a bike ride, swim in the pool, skateboard, sidewalk chalk, basketball, swings, bubbles, etc.

Responsibilities may include: making your bed, sweeping, vacuuming, feeding the family pet, taking out the trash, etc.

On the back of each card is the task analysis for the corresponding activity. It may include such information as where the activity should take place, what materials are needed, what to do if you need help, how long it should take, how you know you are done, and how to clean up.

Your child can choose one activity from each of the three pockets for the afternoon, and put them in the Today pocket. When the activity is finished, the card goes back into its original pocket. Activities can be added or omitted depending on available choices, weather, safety, etc. Reward appropriate transitioning between activities, independence and making choices.

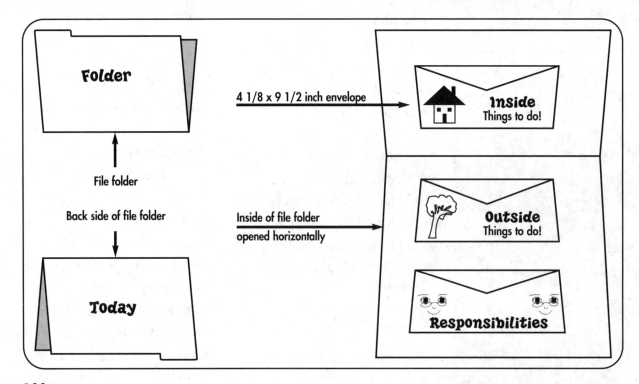

Visual Idea: Play Date Visual

This is a way to visually organize a play date, to help your child know what they can (and should) do on a play date. Provide several options of items that your child likes (these are "Yes" behaviors) and help your child to choose with their friend what they will play. It may be necessary to provide a "reward"/reinforcement for engaging in the play items with their friend. Additionally, you may want to remind your child of a few "No" behaviors or behaviors that are not appropriate to engage in and make your reward contingent on the absence of these behaviors as well.

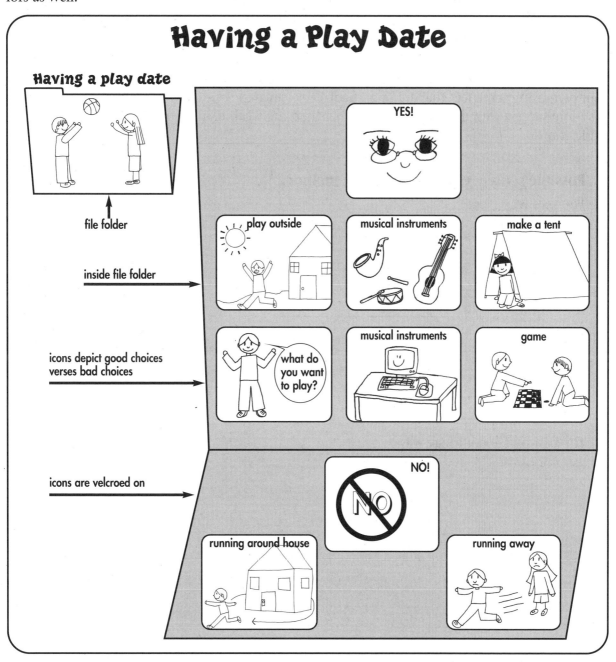

Visual Idea: Today at School

These sheets are for children who need prompting and scripts to engage in a conversation at home about their school day. The child can complete the sheets with the assistance of an aide or teacher throughout the day, after completing each activity, or at the end of the day, with the daily activity schedule readily available for reference. Picture Exchange Communication Symbols (PECS) can be used to complete the worksheet sentences. These may be adhered with Velcro or glue stick.

These three sheets are designed to become gradually more difficult and can be used together for a comprehensive review of your child's day. The sheets use clear language and establish expectations. After all three sheets have been introduced, fade the visual scripts and add more open-ended questions to generate an extended conversation.

Sample visual scripts have been provided for your use. However, you may decide to create your own using sentences that are of particular relevance to your child's day. Perhaps your child has more success with days of the week rather then the weather, use your child's strengths to guide you.

Possible sentences for completion include:

The year is _____

For snack, I ate _____

In gym, I played _____

The month is _____

My job was _____

My friend was _____

For lunch, I ate _____

Today is _____

The weather was _____

The best part about today was _____

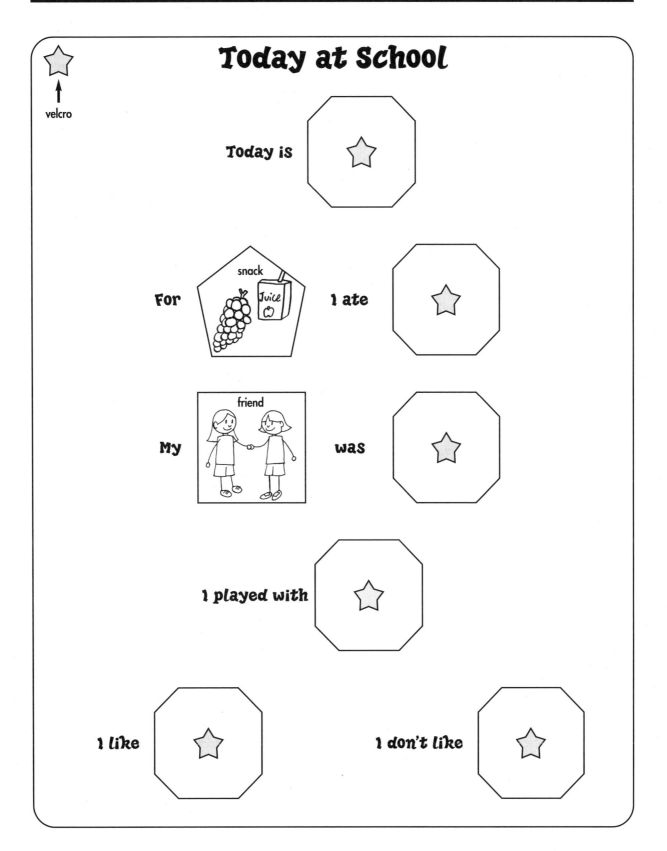

Today at School

velcro

Today is

For <small>snack</small>

I ate

My <small>friend</small>

was

I played with

I like

I don't like

Notes from School

I want to tell you about my day...

In Mr. Smith's class I learned...

_____

_____

_____

_____

In gym class, I played kick ball _____

        tee ball _____

        basketball _____

        _____

At lunch, I sat with _____

_____

At recess, my friends, _____(names) and I played _____

My favorite part of the day was _____

Extra Special Activities _____

Today we had a special thing happen, _____

_____

_____

_____

_____

Teacher's Notes _____

_____

_____

_____

_____

I want to tell you what I did last night...

What did you do last night?
I played _____
I went _____
I saw _____
On TV, I watched _____
What did you have to eat?
For a snack after school, I ate _____
For dinner, I ate _____
For dessert, I had _____
Did you do anything special last night?
A special thing that happened was _____
_____
_____
What did you have for breakfast today?
This morning for breakfast, I ate _____

Conversation Program Ideas

Follow the teaching strategies and teach this series of skills in succession to build a repertoire of conversation skills.

Always:

O Greet others spontaneously, with proper face/body positioning

O Maintain proper body positioning and eye contact

O Develop the conversation process:

Phase 1 – Answers basic social questions ("What is your name?", "How old are you?") and answers basic Yes/No questions, moving to making statements on child's preferred topic.

Phase 2 – Answers Yes/No questions first, then more complex questions on non-preferred topics.

Phase 3 – Contingent commenting. Ex: Parent: "I have a Gameboy." Child comments: "I have one too."

Phase 4 – Comments to others about the activity/game that they are engaged in.

Phase 5 – Expands comments to make contingent statements based on other's topics and continues conversation for extended period of time.

Phase 6 – Initiates new topic ideas.

Phase 7 – Asks other people questions about themselves.

Phase 8 – Compliments others.

Phase 9 – Interrupts or gains appropriate attention when others are speaking.

Phase 10 – End conversations appropriately.

Phase 11 – Generalizes skills to peers.

Phase 1

O Set up the conversation data sheet (next page) with your child. Write the topic at the top (read it to your child, if your child can't read) and then ask 5 questions. Each time he/she answers a yes/no question using proper body positioning as you have reviewed or visually prompted, he/she should get a check mark. When your child gets 5 check marks, change topics. Openly record check marks for your child to see or have your child make check marks for his/herself. Use mastered yes/no questions as you are taking data on body positioning.

O Reverse the process. Let your child pick the conversation topic and ask you the questions. Have your child monitor you for appropriate body positioning, and have him/her give you check marks.

Work on this exercise until your child is consistent with answering questions using appropriate body/face positioning, in a variety of locations, at least 5 times successfully. Then move to Phase 2.

Remember appropriate body/face positioning may include, but is not limited to: making eye contact; sitting with shoulders facing forward; sitting properly on the chair, not facing sideways; not covering mouth.

Phase 2

Involves expanding your questions to more open-ended questions, requiring greater thought. Start by asking your child about topics you are certain they can answer: "What is your favorite video game?", "What is your favorite cartoon?" Then expand the conversation even further.

Conversation Data Sheet

Topic: _____

I

1) Answered yes/no questions

2) Had proper body/shoulder positioning

3) Made eye contact when answering

☐ ☐ ☐ ☐ ☐ Great! 😊

OR

Topic: _____

I

1) Answered basic social questions

2) Had proper body/shoulder positioning

3) Made eye contact when answering

☐ ☐ ☐ ☐ ☐ Great! 😊

Phases 3 and 4 – Expanding Conversation through playing games and making comments during turn-taking

This goal can be worked on at the same time as the other conversation goals.

○ Pick a game that your child enjoys and that requires turn taking. It should last about 15-20 minutes.

○ Help your child accept taking turns and waiting for his/her turn. If he/she needs more then occasional reminders, then create a visual. Write out, "your turn" on an index card and place it in front of the person who's turn it is, moving the visual after each turn. Fade to having the child, whose turn just ended, move the visual to face the child who needs to take a turn. Eliminate prompt when skill is mastered.

○ Model appropriate comments during the game. For example, if you are playing monopoly, comment, "I hope I don't go to jail". Set up a tally sheet to keep track of comments. Set up the occasion for your child to comment after each turn about something that happened to them.

○ Write out comments on an index card or sheet of paper, if your child can read, to use as a visual prompt. Fade these as he/she is more successful.

○ To generalize, add more people to the game, hopefully friends. Provide visual cues as necessary for turn taking and commenting.

Commenting checklist

Sample of comments:

"I like _____ "

"I hope that _____ "

"I am waiting for _____ "

"I don't want _____ "

8-10 comments per game

Note: each box represents a comment card, use cards to prompt, prompt at appropriate intervals, fade prompts quickly.

When game is over:

"Good game, thanks for playing!"

Phase 5 – Topic Maintenance/Contingent Statements

Teach your child to identify the topic in a conversation and make a basic contingent statement. Start talking, and as you talk, hold up a card that lists the topic. For example, say "I went to the beach today" you would hold up the card "beach". Your child is to then comment back. If he/she is not able to comment back about this topic, then set up comment cards for him/her to practice with. Comment cards could look like this:

Sample 1:

Person 1	Student
"I went to the beach"	Comment cards to choose from:
(person holds up beach topic card)	

"I went to the beach too!"	"I didn't go to the beach!"

Sample 2:

Repeat, but now show toys you have

"I have a new Robot"

"I have that too!"	"I don't have that yet!"

Be sure to practice and build up conversation, using the "I like" statements embedded with " I went" and "I have" in your conversations and use the topic comment cards.

Phase 6 – Initiate New Topic

I am going to list my favorite things, then use this to ask my friends if they like it too.

I like:

_____ "Do you?"

_____ "Do you?"

_____ "Do you?"

_____ "Do you?"

Now, I can talk about things that I have, such as a bike and a computer, and ask questions. One question I can ask is:

"Do you have _____?"

I am going to list my favorite things, then use this to ask my friends if the have these things too.

I have:

_____ "Do you?"

_____ "Do you?"

_____ "Do you?"

_____ "Do you?"

Phase 7 – Ask questions

Talk with your friends about things you both like

1) Find things in common: (things you both like)

Here are some questions:

"What is your favorite movie?" _____

"What is your favorite TV show?" _____

"Where do you like to go?" _____

"What is your best subject?" _____

"What subject do you hate the most?" _____

"What are things you don't like?" _____

think of your own question _____

2) Pick your topic in common from above:

Talk about   Talk about

_____   _____

3) Now ask questions:

"Who do you _____ "

"When do you _____ "

"What is your favorite part of _____ "

"Your question idea here: _____ "

Phase 8 – Complimenting others makes them feel good about themselves and makes them enjoy being with you.

○ If your child doesn't understand the importance of giving compliments, use a social story to explain.

○ Once your child has read the social story, set up visual cues for giving compliments.

○ In a role-playing situation, give your child some samples of some compliments that they can give their friends and when it would be appropriate to give that compliment.

○ Initiate complimenting by verbally cueing your child. Say something like, "Her hair looks pretty in a ponytail, doesn't it?" Or model a compliment by saying, "I really like your shoes. Don't you like her shoes?" or (Insert child's name), aren't those nice shoes?

○ Have your child compliment you, across different situations.

○ Have your child practice complimenting other friends and family using both verbal and visual cues, as necessary.

○ Begin to fade the visual by telling your child that he/she has to give a couple of compliments a day to different people across their day.

○ Spend time throughout the session modeling compliments, as well!

○ Teach your child "Thank you" as a response to receiving compliments.

Complimenting Worksheet

Here are some ways to do it:

1) Compliment appearance and/or items they have:
(Examples: haircut, clothes, smile, computer game, book, sneakers)

"I like your _____ "

visual card

2) Compliment something they do well:
(Examples: they are good at games, they are nice, they are good at swimming, etc.)

"You are really good at _____ "
  or "Way to go!"

visual card

3) Compliment something they did for you that you liked:
(Example: helped you with something, gave you something, set something up for you)

"Thank you for _____ "

visual card

When someone gives you a compliment, look at them and say
"Thank you"

Phase 9 – Gaining attention of others

Sometimes, we talk and others get distracted. If we really want to tell them something important, we should work to get their attention.

Model this skill, and then role-play how and when to gain someone's attention.

Here are some suggestions:

O Walk up and talk to your friend. If they are not looking at you, get their attention: tap them on the shoulder, say "Excuse me", or "Hey_____"

O Start talking to your friend. Look at them while you talk to them.

O If your friend stops paying attention to you, try getting their attention:
  — Tap their shoulder
  — Say "Excuse me" or "Hey _____"
  — Look at them and see if they are looking at you.
  — Repeat what you said if they missed it.

Great job!

Phase 10 – Ending Conversations Appropriately

Teaching appropriate conversation endings is important. There are many social rules and situations that apply to conversation endings. Start off by teaching your child how to recognize and end a basic 1:1 conversation.

1:1 Conversation ending:

Step 1: Start by using your conversation data sheet (p. 146).

When you are done with your conversation (and all of the checks are completed):

> **Introduce Ending:**
>
> "Ok, Bye"
>
> "Talk to ya later"
>
> "Gotta go" (etc.)

Step 2: Have a conversation, without the data sheet. Instruct your child to use a conversation ending when you are done talking.

Step 3: Have your child engage in and end a conversation with another person. A way to prompt this: each time the other speaker is done, hold a sign up that indicates a pause in conversation. Your child should recognize the pause as an opportunity to end the conversation. When the pause sign goes up, it's OK for your child to use the conversation ending: "Ok, bye", or "See ya later", or "Talk to you tomorrow". Prior to working on generalization of this skill it may be necessary to advise the conversation partner as to how many exchanges you would like in order to reinforce your child. Gradually increase the exchanges, then vary the exchanges so your child doesn't learn to anticipate a pause and then allow the exchanges to progress naturally.

Step 4: Work on having the conversation flow more naturally. Fade visual cues completely. Pick a topic and talk about it until neither of you can think of anything else to say. If your child doesn't recognize the pause(s) independently, re-introduce the "pause" card visual.

Step 5: Generalize these skills to other adults, and then other peers. When your child can successfully end a conversation, review formal (adults) and informal or friendly endings (friends).

> **Endings with adults:**   "Ok, Bye"
>
>   "Talk to you tomorrow"
>
>   "It was nice talking to you"
>
> **Endings with friends:** "See ya dude"
>
>   "Catch ya later"
>
>   "I'm outta here"

Conversation Visual Idea:

On the walls in Janis' Social Skills room, she has several different simple social skills references, each topic has their own color and shape. The topic is listed in a large shape in the middle, with smaller shapes around it that include simple cues that can be easily referenced throughout the group session. Occasionally, she will copy these visuals for the parents to take home or to take to school as a carry-over activity.

Examples of "wall curriculum" ideas are outlined below:

Look at my partner	**Stand still**	**Hands down**

Having a Conversation

Listen to my partner	**Ask a question**	**Use good talking voice**	**Talk slowly**

Visual Ideas: Self-Regulation

Visual Idea: My Feelings Book:

This book can help students with limited verbal abilities, especially when they are anxious. Work through problem solving to develop and create coping strategies. This book can be used when your child is experiencing frustration or sadness or is very happy or excited about something, but does not have the verbal or behavior skills to express those emotions appropriately. Direct your child to write (with or without varying levels of assistance) about what he/she is feeling. Finish the sentence "I am feeling happy because…" and then "Solution" is a place to create an appropriate coping strategy, developing a good way to show or express that feeling. The book can be used over and over again, using the dry erase markers to create new "feelings and solution stories" as the occasion arises.

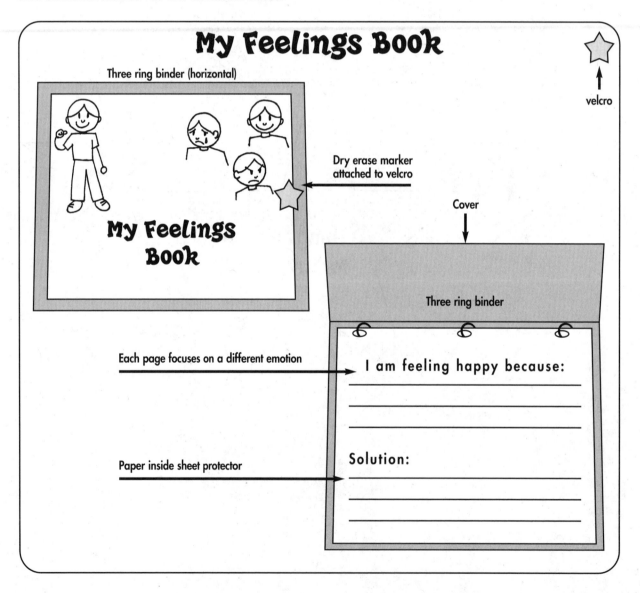

Visual Idea: When I get mad I can...

Visual Idea: Self-Monitoring

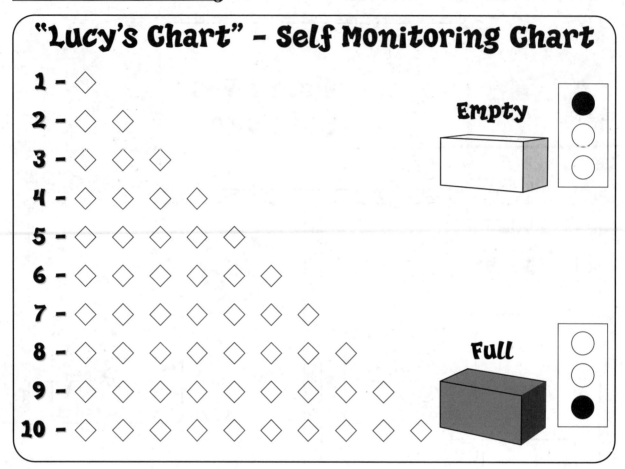

Lucy's Chart: This chart serves a multitude of purposes:

- O It can be used to visually signal voice volume (1= silent, 10=yelling, 4= good inside voice, 5= reading aloud in class, etc.). Use the chart to teach a student about voice volume regulation and control and refer to the chart to non-verbally cue louder or softer voice in social settings.

- O It can be used to signal activity level (calm versus overactive) similar to voice volume mentioned above.

- O It can be used to signal the duration of an activity (1= "Go" 10= "Stop") to let the student know how close he is to completion in the absence of a timer

- O The chart can be used with multi-sensory cues, as well, beads can be used for counters in numbers 1-10, the stop and go traffic light, the full/empty cues, and the 1-10 scale progression of numbers are all commonly used visual and social cues that can be combined into one visual that can easily generalize into other environments and settings.

Visual Idea: What to do with Oh No!

Have this visual ready and rehearse the different relaxation techniques that can be used. Once your child can respond to each one, use this to help determine good choices to relax. The child should have access to a variety of techniques, but should choose the one that is most helpful.

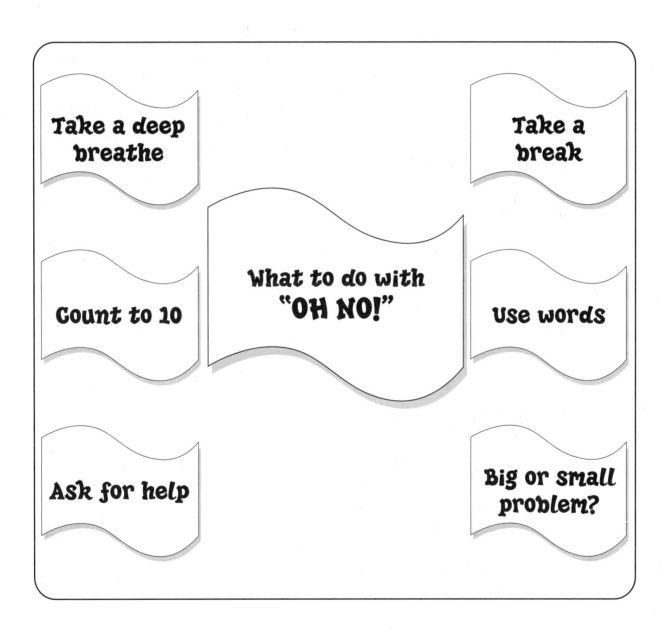

Take a deep breathe

Take a break

Count to 10

What to do with "OH NO!"

Use words

Ask for help

Big or small problem?

Play Station Task Analysis Cards:

These cards outline specific things to do on the playground and "how to" details. These can be used as non-verbal cues and promote independence by teaching your child to follow a structured outline of behavior and language expectations.

Playground Play Stations

3x5 index card

I can:
1) Get on swing
2) Push a friend
3) Ask a friend to push me
4) Take turns
5) Be careful walking near a swing

Swing

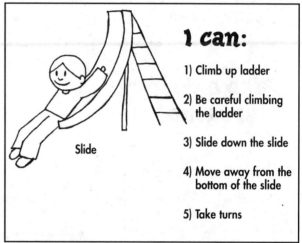

I can:
1) Climb up ladder
2) Be careful climbing the ladder
3) Slide down the slide
4) Move away from the bottom of the slide
5) Take turns

Slide

I can:
1) Ask a friend to play catch with me
2) Take turns
3) Throw the ball to my friend
4) Catch the ball

Catch

I can:
1) Climb on ladders
2) Swing on rings
3) Swing on bars
4) Climb on monkey bars
5) Be careful when I walk under jungle gym

Jungle gym

Visual Idea: Teaching Games:

When teaching games, as we have mentioned before, make sure your child has a good understanding of HOW the game is played first. We have done social stories and scripting, to teach how teams are chosen, what each person in a game does (for instance, if you are playing kickball, explain what "bases" and the "outfield" are) in a picture (or even video) format. Then use a behavior rehearsal technique to practice. Once your child has a general understanding of HOW to play the game, use the visual strategy below to help continue to learn other skills, as well as to self-monitor.

Recess Activity Schedule:

This schedule is to help structure recess time into smaller chunks of time and concrete activities that are familiar to the student. The activity schedule at recess follows the same protocol as a regular activity schedule, but perhaps with shorter segments of time, and with more transitions. Keep in mind that the activity schedule should be introduced at first in short segments of time, with opportunities for a break included in the schedule, and then decrease the number of breaks and increase the activities within the schedule.

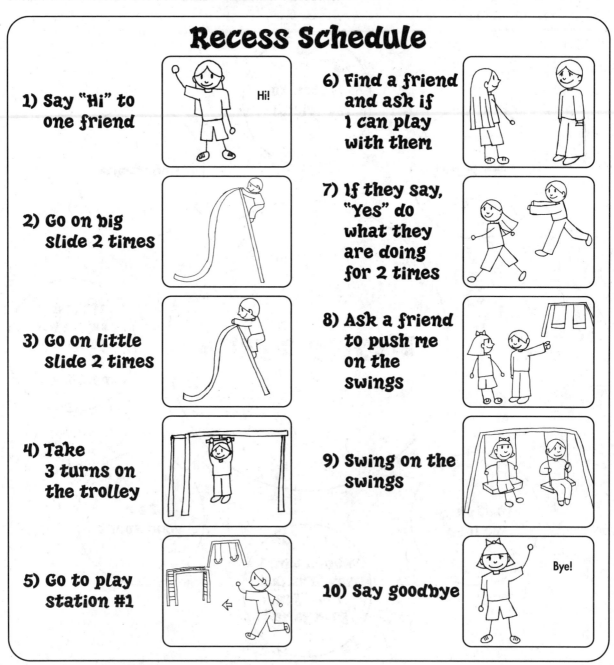

Visual Idea: Recess Log

Some times children know what to do, but don't always do it. It can be helpful to give them cues to help self-monitor their behavior, and provide reinforcement for a job well done and for their behavior.

Recess Log

Find Friends ☐

Join in their play ☐

Play for 15 minutes ☐

Keep my hands to myself ☐

Compliment one friend ☐

Did I do it?   Yes/No

Visual Idea: My Book

This book is a combination activity schedule, self-monitoring book and token reinforcement system all in one! The inside cover of the book has the target rules or behavior expectations for the child; the pages of the book (one per day) outline the daily activities and schedules (wake, get dressed, go to school, doctor's appointments, play date, going to the store, dinner, bed time, movie, etc.). There are corresponding task analysis cards for each activity that has several steps to outline behavior specific steps or behavior expectations or materials needed. (Getting ready for school, the TA card would include: get dressed, make bed, breakfast, brush teeth, comb hair, get backpack, put on shoes, stand near front door.). The child can then be independent to follow the routine (referencing the TA cards if necessary with words or pictures) for each activity. The token system, on the back cover of the book can be used to reinforce target behaviors and compliance to the schedule.

The book is portable and can be used in restaurants, airplanes and in the community. The book is designed to be a reference that can be used in much the same way we use our planners and date books, to help us organize and prioritize our activities and behaviors. The book can also be used as a language tool to talk about what happened yesterday, planning for the future and tracking and reflecting on days of good behavior. The system has been very successful for many students of varying skill levels. The student may need assistance at first to fill out the daily routines, but eventually, the goal is to promote independence in creating and following through on the day's activities.

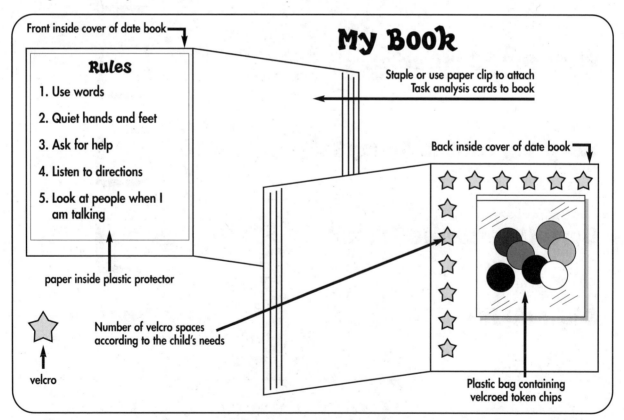

My Book

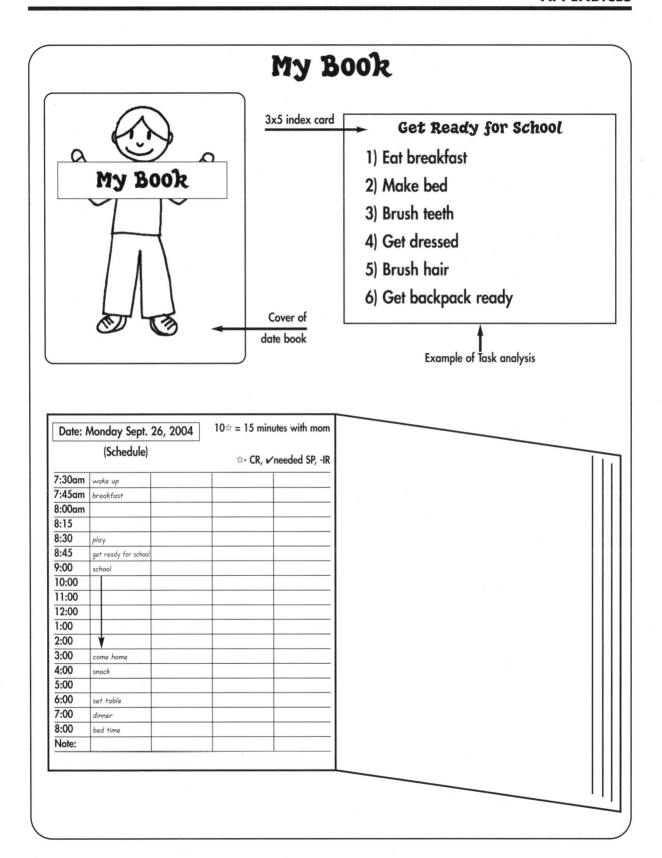

My Book

3x5 index card →

Get Ready for School

1) Eat breakfast
2) Make bed
3) Brush teeth
4) Get dressed
5) Brush hair
6) Get backpack ready

← Cover of date book

↑ Example of Task analysis

Date: Monday Sept. 26, 2004	10☆ = 15 minutes with mom		
(Schedule)	☆- CR, ✔needed SP, -IR		
7:30am	wake up		
7:45am	breakfast		
8:00am			
8:15			
8:30	play		
8:45	get ready for school		
9:00	school		
10:00			
11:00			
12:00			
1:00			
2:00			
3:00	come home		
4:00	snack		
5:00			
6:00	set table		
7:00	dinner		
8:00	bed time		
Note:			

What is a friend?/Making friends.

(start teaching where appropriate with your child)

- O Know how to determine your own likes/dislikes
  — Draw or write a list of them

- O With one other, or a group of students, draw or write your likes/dislikes

- O Pick one of the things that you and one or two other friends liked the same
  — Do that thing you liked the same, together
  — Add in appropriate language to this (see earlier worksheet on commenting to help with this)

- O Pick a new thing you and two other friends liked the same
  — Do that thing
  — Add in appropriate language to this (see earlier worksheet on commenting)
  — Continue with this

- O Try something new with your friend (support your child behaviorally to do this)

- O Read a book about friends (for younger students we recommend the book: **Tobin Learns to Make Friends**, by Diane Murrell, from Future Horizons. This book lists many different skills to being a good friend.).

- O Make a friend book:
  — Pick someone that you have played with and draw, write, or take pictures of you and that friend and what you liked to do the same
  — Set up your book with lots of pictures of you and other friends doing the same things you both like

- O Review the friends rules in the Tobin book (or for older children, set up scenarios on video or make a book) and draw or write about how you obeyed the rules.

Rules for a good friend include:

- Playing the same things/liking the same things
- Sharing with your friend
- Sitting next to or playing next to your friend
- Trading things
- Asking before borrowing
- Walking with your friend, not ahead or behind
- Noticing your friend needs help and helping them
- Complimenting your friends (using nice words)
- Noticing your friends emotions, helping them or saying nice things about them
- Inviting a friend to play with you
- Inviting a friend to come to your house to play with you, or go somewhere with you
- Calling a friend on the phone

○ Set up scenarios and role-play these rules with your friend, so you have a good understanding of each one. You can also add these to your friend book with drawings or lists of each rule and how you/child will follow through with each rule.

○ Use your friend chart and set up different times you can seek out your friend, or play with your friend.

○ Work on identifying different emotions, and how to respond. Add these to your friends book.

○ Use the friend book (pictures or lists) to help as a teaching tool or as a visual self-monitoring form or reminder list.

○ Learn some jokes. Add these to your friend list and keep them handy to use, friends love to laugh and have fun together!

○ Set up play dates, ask a friend over to play. Use the play date visual to help organize and structure this so it goes well.

Buddy Center Worksheets

Find Out About a Friend:
Fill out this form and trade with a friend to compare!

My name is _____

I live in _____

I have _____ sisters and _____ brothers

I have _____ pets. They are _____ .
Their names are: _____

My favorite thing to eat is _____

My favorite thing to play is _____

My favorite movie/TV show is _____

My favorite part of school is _____

My favorite thing to do after school is _____

I am really good at _____

You can ask me about _____

Find friends that like the same things and do them together!

Things our class is good at _____

_____   _____

_____   _____

_____   _____

_____   _____

_____   _____

_____   _____

_____   _____

_____   _____

_____   _____

_____   _____

List or draw below.

Things We Like:

_____ | _____
(name student #1) | (name student #2)

I like: | **I like:**

Things We Don't Like:

_____ | _____
(name student #1) | (name student #2)

I don't like: | **I don't like:**

Things we have in common!

We both like:

We both don't like:

Do we make good friends?

Visual Idea: Safe/Unsafe

This chart outlines visually, target behaviors for certain situations. Other ideas include: When I am talking to my friends (good choices and bad choices), When I don't understand something in class, When I need help, When I want to play with a friend, etc.

Program Forms:

○ **Social Skill Program Form**

○ **Home Communication Form**

○ **Sample Data Sheet**

○ **Sample permission form for peers**

○ **Sample certificate of gratitude-thanks to our peers**

The Social Skills Program

Child/Group name: _____

SAMPLE STRATEGIES

*choose from modules

ACTIVITY	SKILL TARGET	DATA COLLECTION TARGET SKILLS OBSERVED YES/NO	PROMPT LEVEL
Arrival			
Snack			

The Social Skills Program

Child/Group name: _____

SAMPLE STRATEGIES

*choose from modules

ACTIVITY	SKILL TARGET	DATA COLLECTION TARGET SKILLS OBSERVED YES/NO	PROMPT LEVEL
Let's Talk			
Let's Play			
Let's Be Funny			

The Social Skills Program - Home Communications

Child/Group name: _____ date _____

1) Today we worked on:

_____

2) What you should practice:

_____

3) Possible play dates and ideas:

_____

4) Suggestions for community goals:

_____

Please contact us with questions

_____

(use this during your social skills teaching)

Social Skills Solutions

Data Collection Record

Group: _____

Student: _____

Date: _____

Student: _____

Date: _____

Skill Target _____
SD: _____
R: _____
_____

Skill Target _____
SD: _____
R: _____
_____

Skill Target _____
SD: _____
R: _____
_____

Skill Target _____
SD: _____
R: _____
_____

Skill Target _____
SD: _____
R: _____
_____

Skill Target _____
SD: _____
R: _____
_____

(use this to formally track all of your skills)

Social Skills Solutions

Data/Progress Record

Student: _____

Clinician: _____

Date(s) *Social Skills Checklist* Completed:

Initial: _____

Update: _____

Update: _____

Update: _____

Target skills:	Session #1	Session #2	Session #3	Session #4	Session #5	Session #6	Session #7	Session #8	Session #9	Session #10
Level: Module: Skill:	Record current skill level including prompts For each session →									
Level: Module: Skill:										
Level: Module: Skill:										
Level: Module: Skill:										
Level: Module: Skill:										
Level: Module: Skill:										

Sample permission slip for groups

Dear Parents,

Your child _____ *has been recommended as a peer role model for a class that teaches children how to play, interact, and socialize properly. The group has four students that need to learn these skills, three adults and will need four children to serve as role models.*

Your child is a wonderful role model for these skills! The group will meet at _____.

A snack will be provided. Please sign below if you give us permission to have your child be a role model in this group.

We look forward to working with your child. Please call if you have any further questions.

Sincerely,

_____

Student name _____   *Class teacher* _____

Yes, I give my child _____ *permission to participate in this after school social skills class.*

No, my child _____ *cannot participate in this class at this time.*

_____

Parent/Guardian signature   *Date*

SAMPLE CERTIFICATE FOR PEERS

Certificate of gratitude and completion:

_____

**has participated in the peer model
Social Skills Learning Program**

Thank you for your support!

_____

(name, date)

GLOSSARY OF COMMONLY USED TERMS

ABC Chart: This form allows you to document the occurrence of antecedents, problem behavior, and consequences that immediately follow problem behavior. "A" refers to antecedent, which means the stimulus that immediately precedes a problem behavior. The "B" refers to the behavior that is observed and "C" refers to the consequence, which is the stimulus that follows the response

Adaptive: Behavior that results in a reinforcing outcome or serves a specific purpose

Advocacy Organization: A group of people working on behalf of people with disabilities, their families, and individuals who support them

Antecedent: A stimulus (i.e. a verbal cue, activity, event or person) that immediately precedes a behavior. This stimulus may or may not serve as discriminative for a specific behavior

Antecedent-Behavior-Consequence (ABC) Analysis: A description of the antecedents and consequences associated with targeted behaviors to identify what variables reliably predict and maintain targeted behavior

Antecedent-Related Interventions: The modification of events that immediately precede problem behaviors. Examples include changes in the physical setting, curriculum, or schedule

Assessment: The process of gathering information in order to make a decision about what actions should be taken.

Baseline: An initial data record of a target behavior's occurrence. A baseline is used to compare the initial data to the data collected after an intervention is implemented.

Baseline Condition: A phase conducted during an experiment where the independent variable, an event or variable manipulated by a researcher, is absent.

Behavior Consultant: A professional with a background in applied behavior analysis whose expertise is in using this principle of learning to teach skills and manage (increase or decrease target) behaviors. Behavior Consultants can vary in levels of training and experience and areas of expertise; they can work within an organization or be hired temporarily.

Behavior Support Plan: A written and agreed upon set of strategies developed to increase or decrease specified target behaviors. Behavioral support plans contain multiple intervention strategies designed to modify the environment and teach new skills.

Behavioral Definition: A statement that identifies an action or response in clear and explicit terms and allows one to measure its occurrence.

Case Manager: A professional who serves as a point of contact for an individual with disabilities or their family. This person seeks out and coordinates resources, monitors progress, and communicates with the individual, family, and all professionals involved.

Chaining: an instructional procedure that organizes the individual responses in a sequence, to complete a complex behavior, such as hand washing or cleaning a room.

Coercion Theory: Coercive interactions develop between two people when one person engages in a negative behavior to achieve a social outcome and the other person responds in an equally negative fashion. The ongoing exchange between the two individuals increases in intensity until one of them gives up. The origin of this hypothesis is associated with G. Patterson and M. Sidman.

Communication: The set of skills that enables a person to convey information so that it is received and understood.

Consequence: A response (i.e. a verbal response, the acquisition or withholding of a reinforcing item or activity) that follows a behavior. For instance, if a little girl's crying results in attention from her teacher, then the teacher's attention would be considered a consequence that followed the crying behavior. Also, if a child says "I love you" to his/her mother, and the mother hugs her child, her hug is a consequence.

Consequence Interventions: Strategies used to affect the outcome or occurrence of appropriate behaviors. Two strategies can be used when problem behaviors occur more frequently than appropriate behavior: increase reinforcement for appropriate behavior, and decrease reinforcement received for engaging in problem behavior.

Continuous reinforcement: The positive act or process of presenting a stimulus for every correct/desired response in an effort to insure a re-occurrence of the specified response. Effective in teaching a new skill/behavior.

Correlation: When two or more variables occur together it indicates the likelihood of a common relationship or interaction between those variables.

Data Collection: Recording objective and measurable observations including but not, limited to rate, frequency and duration of behaviors/skills. Different types of data collecting include: Frequency: recording the number of times a behavior occurs; interval recording: the observation time is divided into equal amounts of time and behavior is recorded as occurred/not occurred during each interval; duration: recording the length of time from when a targeted behavior begins until its termination; Latency: recording the time between the presentation of the stimulus/instructional cue and the occurrence of the response from the individual; Task analysis recording: recording performance on steps of a task analysis to determine strengths/deficits within the task.

Developmental Disability: any severe or chronic, mental, physical, emotional or cognitive impairment (or combination of impairments) resulting in substantial functional limitations in three or more of the following areas of major life activity: self-care, receptive and expressive language, learning, mobility, self-direction, capacity for independent living, and economic self-sufficiency. Common developmental disabilities include mental retardation, autism, and cerebral palsy, among others

Direct Observation: Watching the individual in order to clearly identify when problem behaviors occur, what happens right before, what the problem behaviors looks like, and how the behaviors are responded to. Direct observation can help you develop a hypothesis statement about why problem behaviors occur, and confirm or disprove this hypothesis.

Discrete Trial: A teaching method that presents a stimulus or instruction, designed to illicit a targeted response, which is followed by a prompt or reinforcer depending on the accuracy of the response.

Disruptive Behavior: An individual's action or response that interferes with learning. Minor disruptive behaviors include talking out of turn, not paying attention, or refusing to work on in-class assignments. Severe disruptive behaviors include aggression, self-injury, property destruction, and screaming.

Duration: The time elapsed between the beginning and ending of a targeted event; how long a behavior lasts.

Empowerment and control: The perception that one is in charge of his or her destiny. Giving persons with disabilities opportunities to make choices in their life by using their own judgment and discretion on a daily basis.

Endogenous Opiates: Commonly associated with "runner's high." An internally produced (within the brain or other body tissue) morphine-like substance that results in a feeling of euphoria.

Environmental Events: The physical setting, routines, activities, and individuals surrounding an individual.

Errorless Teaching: A method of instruction that teaches a new skill with the necessary prompts/supports in place to be sure that an error in response does not occur and thus, no patterns of error are established.

Fading or Prompt Fading: A systematic process of gradually eliminating a prompt or an assistance stimulus, from the most to the least invasive. The idea is that the response begins to occur automatically and independently in the presence of the learned stimuli without any assistance from the instructor.

Frequency: The number of times a behavior occurs in a specified observation period.

Function: The reason why a particular behavior occurs. Documented functions of problem behavior include (a) getting attention, (b) desire for activities or items, (c) escape from attention or activities, and (d) escape from or to obtain physiological stimulation.

Functional Analysis: Determining the relationship between the occurrence of problem behavior, the antecedent, and the consequence through direct observation and the systematic manipulation of environmental events.

Functional Assessment: Also known as Functional Behavioral Assessment. The process of collecting information in order to develop hypothesis statements regarding the variables that maintain and predict problem behavior. Functional assessment strategies include indirect assessment methods, direct observation, and functional analysis.

Hypothesis Statement: A statement that is based on observation and attempts to predict an outcome. A hypothesis statement provides information about how environmental events affect the likelihood of behaviors, which environmental events precede behaviors, and what is the probable function of these behaviors.

IDEA: Individuals with Disabilities Education Act and the parallel statutes of many states guarantees the right to a free and appropriate public education in the least restrictive environment for students with disabilities. Should the local school district be unable to provide this education, they are responsible for finding a facility that can provide one for your child. The law applies to all students between the ages of 3 and 21 who qualify for special education and related services. Local school districts are held responsible for identification and initial evaluation of each student and interdisciplinary teams work with the individual and parents to generate an annual individualized education plan (IEP).

IEP: Individual Education Plan. A legal document that is developed by the individual's team to determine an individual's specific educational needs and goals and any special modifications necessary for the upcoming year.

Incidental teaching: Teaching that occurs as a result of a spontaneous or unexpected event in which a desired response is elicited and can be reinforced with natural contingencies and reinforcements or with pre-existing rewards (tokens, etc.).

Inclusion Facilitator: A school staff person who assists regular and special education teachers, including students with disabilities, into regular education classrooms within the regular education curriculum. This person often has a background in special education and may be a resource to general educators on matters pertaining to special education, environmental and curricular modifications, and IDEA.

Indirect Assessment Strategies: Gathering information about an individual and the behaviors of concern from reports of people who know the individual. Interviews, record reviews, quality of life measures, checklists, and rating scales about the individual's behavior are all considered indirect ways of obtaining information. These strategies are often the initial step taken in the functional assessment process.

Interdisciplinary Team: The people from different perspectives or disciplines that join together to problem solve and develop educational and behavior plans. Team members may include the individual, parent(s) or other family members, teachers, occupational/physical therapists, medical doctors, psychologists, consultants, specialists, community members, job coaches, vocational rehabilitation counselors, and paraprofessionals.

Inter-observer Agreement: When data is recorded by two or more sources separately, documenting the same behavior to assure that a measurement system has a certain level of accuracy. This may also be referred to as inter-observer reliability.

Interval: A finite predetermined period of time for the purpose of measurement.

Interval Recording: An observational notation system that takes a predetermined period of time and divides it into equal shorter periods of time in which a behavior is measured.

Latency: The amount of time between the stimulus and a behavior. For example the time between a request (please put on your shoes) and the action (putting on shoes).

Maintaining Consequence: The specific stimulus that occurs contingently upon the presence of problem behavior.

Motivational States: A condition of being moved to action. Four motivational states that have been determined as important in analyzing behavior: attempts to access attention, attempts to escape or avoid; attempts to access tangibles, self-stimulatory or internal feedback.

Multi-component Intervention Plan: A comprehensive use of a variety of strategies that address problem behaviors.

Observational Learning: A method of obtaining information through studying another individual engaged in a behavior.

Off-Task Behavior: The action or response of an individual when he/she is not engaged in or working on a pre-selected task or activity.

On-Task Behavior: The action or response of an individual when he/she is engaged in or working on a specific task or activity.

Outcomes: The results of an intervention. In positive behavioral support, desired outcomes include an improved quality of life in addition to reductions in problem behavior. Outcomes should be defined and agreed upon before the implementation of behavioral support for the proper support to be chosen and to determine when the intervention has met its intended goal.

PBS (Positive Behavioral Support): A comprehensive set of strategies that are meant to redesign environments in such a way that problem behaviors are prevented or inconsequential, and to facilitate the individual's learning new skills, making problem behaviors unnecessary.

Paraphrase: To restate or reword something that has been said by another person in order to confirm your understanding of the information.

Paraprofessional: A teaching assistant usually connected with a special education classroom or student who needs intensive individual support in a regular education classroom.

Person-Centered Plan (Planning): The process of gathering information and goal development that has an individualized focus. The person for whom the planning is done is present at the meeting and the input from that person guides or directs the planning process.

Physical Features of the Environment: Elements of the environment which are experienced by physical means. This includes sights (colors of walls), sound (noise levels), smell (paint), and other features such as temperature, number of individuals in a room, and seating arrangement.

Positive Lifestyle: The result of eliminating or decreasing problem behavior due to increased opportunities for individuals to exercise choice, experience positive social interactions, and to experience stable and predictable environments.

Positive Social Interaction: When two or more people have a discussion or exchange that results in a successful experience for all parties.

Primary Communication: An individual's preferred method of successfully conveying information so that it is received and understood by others.

Principles of Human Behavior: rules or standards that represent the relationship between behavior and the variables that control it. Examples of behavioral principles include reinforcement, punishment, extinction, and stimulus control.

Problem Solving: A systematic approach of utilizing multiple perspectives to dissect the issues related to a particular difficulty, so that an intervention plan can be created and the outcome can be evaluated.

Prompting: Instructional technique that facilitates the correct response. This can include physical, gestural, visual, verbal prompting, or any combination of these.

Punisher: A consequent stimulus that reduces the probability of a behavior occurring.

Quality of Life Measures: A means of assessing an individual's daily living for predictability, environmental stability, level of social belonging, empowerment and control, well-being and satisfaction.

Recording Forms: The data sheets that observers use to document the information gathered from formal observations.

Rehearsal Strategies: the planned opportunity to teach and practice a skill in a setting other then which it should occur (especially if there is a history of negative behaviors) to reduce potential errors in the targeted setting.

Reinforcement: The act or process of presenting or receiving a stimulus that when presented immediately following a response increases the probability that the response will occur again. Can be the presentation of a something pleasant or removal of something unpleasant.

Reinforcer: A stimulus that has been determined to be positive, highly desirable and motivating so that when presented immediately following a response increases the probability that the targeted response will occur again.

Reinforcement schedule: The systematic planning of delivery of a stimulus for the occurrence of desired behavior or for the absence of targeted behavior.

Replacement Behavior: A socially acceptable alternative response that results in the same functional outcome as the problem behavior.

Scatter Plot: An interval recording method where data is recorded during specific time or activity periods.

Setting Event: Any occurrence that affects an individual's response to reinforcement and punishers in the environment. Environmental, social, or physiological factors can all contribute to a setting event.

Setting Event Interventions: Identifying and modifying social, environmental, and physiological factors to temporarily alter the value of reinforcers and punishers within the individual's environment. Interventions may involve minimizing the likelihood of the setting event, changing expectations on days when setting events occur, or neutralizing the setting event.

Shaping: Reinforcing successive approximations towards a desired response. Shaping is used to teach a new behavior by manipulating the consequences presented.

Social Belonging: The feeling of interdependence and connectedness that results from close relationships within a community or other social network. A sense of being part of a group of people, a family, or a team is an important human experience that many individuals consider an important quality of life issue.

Social Network: A web of interconnected people who directly or indirectly interact with or influence your child and family. May include but is not limited to extended family, teachers and other school staff, friends, neighbors, community contacts, and professional support.

Stimulus: Anything that elicits or evokes action or creates a response.

System: A set of related or interacting variables, which function together for a specific purpose. Systems are dynamic and often change over time.

Tactile Stimulation: Eliciting a response by means of touching or through the sense of touch.

Topography: The physical movements or description of a motor behavior.

Variable: That which is changeable and interacts to directly or indirectly alter the outcome.

Visual Picture Schedule: Information regarding the sequence of events or routines your child will be engaging in throughout the day. A schedule may use words, photographs or drawings to convey this information and is a method of providing a sense of predictability and control over environment.

RESOURCES

A brief literature review on social skills

A brief literature review on social skills

We think "social skills" can be defined by the way in which we interact with other people in our environment and world. But how do we do that? How do we break it down? How do we teach that? In exploring these questions, we spent some time reading through some of the current literature and reference materials. We have listed here some of our favorites. These very talented and knowledgeable individuals have inspired us to create this book, which springs from their ideas and dedication to the field of autism.

A landmark book by Dr. Tony Attwood, Asperger's Syndrome: A Guide for Parents and Professionals (1998) noted many strategies for improving skills and social behaviors. There are several chapters that outline general teaching strategies in areas of: social play, codes of conduct, expanding flexibility, cooperation and sharing, eye contact and understanding emotions. We highly recommend reading this book, especially when working with older children on the spectrum.

Another valuable book in the area of social skills is Dr. Kathleen Quill's book Do-Watch-Listen-Say, (2000). This very comprehensive and well-researched book explains the complexities of autism, and in particular how these complexities affect core skills for social and communication development. She notes that there is a "growing understanding that an inability to process and understand social and affective information in a cohesive manner may lie at the core of autism" (referencing Baron-Cohen, 1995; Frith, 1989; Hobson, 1996).

Dr. Quill lists core skills to be considered while looking at social and communication skills for children with autism. Categories assessed include: social behavior, communicative behavior, exploratory behavior, nonverbal and social interaction, imitation-motor/verbal, organization, play, group skills, basic communicative functions, socio-emotional skills-feelings, pro-social statements, basic conversation skills.

The assessment list in this book, and the research and explanation behind the list is one of the most comprehensive assessments we have found. We suggest this book to families and providers working with younger children, as many of the skills in the checklist are appropriate for preschool and early elementary.

A recent publication by Ms. Michelle Garcia-Winner, M.A., S.L.P.-CCC, Inside Out, What Makes A Person With Social Cognitive Deficits Tick, (2000) targets interventions for Asperger's Syndrome, high-functioning autism, Non-verbal Learning Disability (NLD) and PDD students.

In this manual, Ms. Garcia-Winner takes a look at some of the "higher level" social pragmatic processes involved in social skills. Chapters in this manual include: problem solving, initiation, abstract and inferential language, perspective taking and gestalt processing.

Navigating the Social World, a Curriculum for Individuals with Asperger's Syndrome, High

Functioning Autism and Related Disorders, by Dr. Jeanette McAffee (and foreword by Tony Attwood, 2002) is a recently published social skills curriculum.

The curriculum in the book is comprised of social skills curriculum including: recognizing and coping with emotions (recognizing, labeling, expressing, and self-monitoring), communication and social skills (including nonverbal and contextual clues, greetings and goodbyes, initiating conversation, tone of voice, manners, introductions, offering and asking help, giving and receiving compliments, and resolving conflicts) and abstract thinking skills.

This resource suggests many effective ways to teach the social skills that have been mentioned above, particularly for higher-functioning children that have already developed strong play and language repertoires.

Where do we go from here?

While doing our literature and curriculum review, we found that even in all of these manuals social skills meant many different things to many different people. Different assessment tools, educational testing, and current curriculum outlined different areas, and even different philosophies of social skills.

We feel that ALL of the social skills areas noted above are important and relevant. It is for this reason that we have put together our manual. We feel that all of these social skills need to be more concretely defined, be specifically and systematically taught and evaluated, and be immediately targeted for generalization programming and daily use. The skills that are priority to teach are those that would be most often used during the day—the most effective and functional.

We offer up a word of advice when determining appropriate curriculum: when looking at what skills to teach, ability levels, not just age level should be considered. Examining current language skills, motor skills, cognitive skills, and behavior baseline will provide invaluable information in creating an effective and appropriate goal plan.

Social Skills Resources
Books we like about social skills or have referenced:

O   Activity Schedules for Children with Autism. Lynn McClannahan, Ph.D, & Patricia J. Krantz, Ph.D.; W; Woodbine House Publishing
We like this book because it helps breakdown the importance of using a visual schedule with children to foster greater independent work/play. From this book, you can get a lot more uses for picture schedules, including recess schedules and game schedules.

O   Asperger's Syndrome, A Guide for Parents and Professionals.
Tony Attwood, Future Horizons
This is a great book- and one of the first books that had a fairly comprehensive look at social skills, to include many levels/areas of social needs for children, regarding play, language, following rules and making friends.

O   A Work in Progress, Behavior Management Strategies and Curriculum for Intensive Behavioral Treatment of Autism. Ron Leaf, John McEachin; DRL Books, L.L.C.
In this manual, some play and some social conversation for children are referenced in their teaching curriculum.

O   Behavioral Intervention For Young Children With Autism. a manual for parents and professionals, Catherine Maurice, Gina Green, Stephen Luce; Pro-ed publishing
In this manual, some play is referenced in the skills curriculum, as well as a chapter on school inclusion that is very helpful to read.

O   Comic Strip Conversations. Gray, Carol. (1994). Arlington, Texas: Future Horizons Publishers.
This book is a useful tool for working with students with autism and Asperger's syndrome. It provides clear outlines of how and why comic strip conversation panels can be useful for some students with difficulty understanding social interactions and expectations.

O   Do-Watch-Listen-Say, Social and Communication Intervention for Children with Autism. Kathleen Ann Quill; Paul H. Brookes Publishing Co.
Kathy Quill continues to contribute greatly to the autism world in this book. It is a long read, but help explains many important elements of autism, including the difficulty children have with attending to/selecting relevant social cues. The assessment tool has some play and social skills that are relevant to young children.

O   Hands on Manual, A Tool for Teaching Children with Autism. Kelly McKinnon, M.A. Self-published. www.kellymckinnon.com
A beginning tool for parents, that lists many areas of social skills needs, with skills checklists and some teaching strategies for these skills.

○ Inclusive Programming for Elementary Students with Autism and
Inclusive Programming for Middle School Students with Autism. Sheila Wagner, M.A. (2002) Future Horizons.
Sheila Wagner was awarded Autism Society of America,s Literary Work of the Year 2001 for her book on inclusion. This is another book in that series, but the all of them are excellent resources for supporting students in an inclusion setting.

○ Inside Out: What Makes a Person with Social Cognitive Deficits Tick. Michelle Garcia Winner; Michelle Garcia Winner Published, mwinner@world.att.net.
This book is geared toward older children on the spectrum. Michelle, along with many speech and language pathologists help us to look at the importance of teaching children to really listen, think, and problem solve, as a method for teaching social language pragmatics. Book has some worksheets you can use.

○ Navigating the Social World, a curriculum for individuals with Asperger,s Syndrome, High functioning autism and related disorders. Jeanette McAfee, M.D., Future Horizons, 2002.
This is a definitive program with forms, exercises and guides for the students. The curriculum is based on teaching conversation and politeness, and deals with some other areas of behavior. It has a foreword by Tony Attwood, and is geared toward teaching older children.

○ No-Glamour Language. LinguiSystems.
This manual is filled with very helpful worksheets for children, particularly in the areas of social and language pragmatics, and problem solving skills. Topic areas include: predicting, getting the main idea, comparing, synonyms and riddles. Very useful!

○ Play and Imagination in Children with Autism. Wolfberg, Pamela. (1999). New York: Teachers College Press.
Ms. Wolfberg has done a remarkable job in combining research and practical intervention strategies and examples in play with children with autism. This book explores play itself through childhood, and then looks closely at the diagnosis of autism. From this perspective, we are better able to direct play interaction interventions because play itself within typical populations is thoroughly examined. There are several helpful vignettes, case studies and illustrations to provide examples to supplement the research and theory. Also see more current Peer Play and the Autism Spectrum.

○ Reaching Out, Joining In, Teaching Social Skills to Young Children with Autism. Mary Jane Weiss, Ph.D, Sandra L. Harris, Ph.D.; Woodbine House Publishing.
This book is a good first social skills reference for parents and professionals. It has a great section on breaking down perspective taking into many different prerequisite steps to explore before moving ahead.

○ <u>Right From the Start, Behavioral Intervention for Young Children with Autism, A Guide for Parents and Professionals</u>. Sandra L. Harris, Ph.D, & Mary Jane Weiss, Ph.D.; Woodbin House Publishing.
This book is a good reference point for parents to look at the importance of using an ABA approach to teach many skills, including social skills.

○ <u>Skill Streaming the Elementary School Child</u> and <u>Skill Streaming The Adolescent</u>. McGinnis, E. & Goldstein, Arnold. (1997). Illinois: Research Press.
These books address the social skills needs of students who display aggression, immaturity, withdrawal or other problem behaviors.

○ <u>Social Skills Activities for Secondary Students with Special Needs</u>. Darlene Mannix, Prentice Hall Publishers, 1998.
This is a book for student,s in grades 6-12 and contains 187 worksheets that teach students how to apply social skills to real life. It covers listening to others, understanding viewpoints, negotiating or compromising, assessing moods, and dealing with teasing.

○ <u>Teaching Language to Children with Autism or Other Developmental Disabilities</u>. Mark Sundberg & James Partington; Behaviorist Analyst Inc. Publishing.
The ABLLS curriculum and other verbal behavior literature are helpful to look at when working with children with little-to-no functional language.

○ <u>Teach Me Language</u>. Sabrina Freeman Ph.D, Lorelei Dake, B.A., SKF Books.
Although this book is geared mostly for older children, and children with some functional language, there are some good worksheets on teaching social conversation.

○ <u>Teaching Playskills to Children with Autism Spectrum Disorder</u>. Melinda Smith, M.D., (2001). DRL Books, Inc.
This book, along with her website, lists very helpful interventions to teach play at all levels. It is written in a very easy to follow and easy to implement step by step format including which toys to use and what instructions to give your child.

○ <u>Teaching Students with Autism to Mind-Read: A Practical Guide</u>. Howlin, Patricia., Baron-Cohen, Simon., Hadwin, Julie. (1999). New York: John Wiley & Sons.
This book is one-of –a-kind in its theory. Research from these authors is widely respected and this book represents a practical approach to intervention strategies from their years of research and theory. Specific teaching activities and intervention techniques are outlined and examples are provided, along with data collection strategies.

○ <u>Teaching Your Child the Language of Social Success</u>. Duke, M., Nowicki, S. & Martin ,E. (1996). Atlanta, GA: Peachtree Publishers.
This is a great resource for teachers and parents who are looking for a clear and simple approach to defining individual social skills and prerequisite skills for pro-social behavior.

o The Language of Perspective Taking. Marilyn M. Toomey, Circuit Publications, 2002.
This book, also written by a speech and language pathologist, has some helpful worksheets to supplement your work with children and teaching perspective taking. It starts at a mid-level: a child needs to have some prerequisite skills already in place, but the book helps the child to look at emotions, and through worksheets how different people may view things differently.

o Trevor Trevor. Diane Twachtman-Cullen. (1998). Starfish Presses.
This is a good book to read to other children to help children understand and accept the child with autism.

Other helpful books:

o A Handbook of Autism and Pervasive Developmental Disorders. Cohen, Donald, and Volkmar, Fred. (1998) New York: John Wiley & Sons, Inc.
This book is a significant and comprehensive resource for professionals and educators. It clearly and completely presents the latest research and thought about the many facets of the diagnoses on the autism/PDD spectrum. It also presents an evolution of the research within each of the areas of the diagnosis, including language and communication, cognition, learning skills, social skills, etc.

o An Activity Based Approach to Early Intervention. Bricker, Diane., Pretti-Frontczak, Kristie., McComas, Natalya. (1998). Baltimore, Maryland: Paul Brookes Publishing.
This book is very helpful to professionals and teachers working with young students with autism in both a home and center based setting. There are several ideas for a pragmatic approach to intervention for young learners that can be easily implemented.

o Assertive Discipline for Parents. Canter, Lee., Canter, Marlene. (1988). New York, New York: Harper & Row Publishers.
This book is useful for professionals working with parents who have typical children as well as a child with a disability and are looking for intervention strategies that can be easily generalized to siblings. The strategies are behaviorally based, and provide a "typical" and common sense perspective on behavior management.

o Autism: Explaining the Enigma. Frith, U. (1989). Massachusetts: Blackwell Publishers.
This book gives an extremely readable history of autism. It also gives a thorough overview of the latest research and theories. This book presents a psychological perspective of what happens in the autistic mind.

o Behavior Modification: Basic Principles. 2nd ed. Axelrod, S. & Hall R.V. (1999). Texas: Pro-Ed.
This book supplements the behavior management series, giving an overview of behavioral principles. It provides clear examples of how to use these principles in teaching. It breaks down the common terms used within this method of teaching into easy to understand paragraphs defining

each concept. This book would be extremely useful for someone that was beginning to work with autistic individuals, such as teaching assistants or paraprofessionals.

○ Children with Autism- A Parent's Guide. Powers, M. Ed. (1989). Maryland: Woodbine House.
This book is filled with quotes and comments from parents. This is a book for parents that is centered on giving the reader strategies to cope and ways to adapt one's life around the diagnosis. It gives advice on what to look for in programs such as a residential facility. It also includes a thorough index for the reader to quickly access the information that they need and a vast resource guide that is broken down state by state.

○ Educating Children with Autism, National Research Council (2001). National Academy Press.
This book was put together at the request of the U.S. Department of Education's Office of Special Education Programs. The primary focus of the charge was early intervention, preschool and school programs designed for children with autism from birth to age 8. This book reports on the committee's key conclusions and recommendations.

○ Functional Assessment and Program Development for Problem Behavior, A Practical Handbook. O'Neil, Robert., Horner, Robert., Albin, Richard., Sprague, Jeffery., Storey, Keith., Newton, J. Stephan. (1997).Pacific Grove, California: Brooks Publishing Co.
This book is a wonderful resource for professionals and teachers who are developing support plans for their special needs students. It provides clear outlines of procedures as well as reproducible data collection sheets and questionnaires. This book is extremely helpful in educating the novice professional about the entire functional assessment process, from initial interview to implementation techniques.

○ Homework Without Tears. Canter, Lee., Canter, Marlene. (1987). New York, New York: Harper & Row Publishers.
This book is very helpful for professionals working with parents and children who are experiencing difficulty generalizing success in work habits from school to home settings. This book provides support and practical suggestions for working with parents and students, typical or special needs, to develop a home program that successfully creates and maintains structure and organization for the student.

○ Mapping the Mind. Carter, R. (1998). University of California Press, Ltd. London.
This book is a wonderful visual resource for professionals that are learning about the neuro-physiology of the brain and thought and behavior, typical and pathological are rooted in brain activity and function.

○ Reaching the Autistic Child: A Parent Training Program. Kozloff, Martin A. (1998). Cambridge, Massachusetts: Brookline Books.
This book is for professionals who are creating a parent training component to their program for

*children with autism. It is very informative, although very technical and written for the profes-
sional with a background and working knowledge of the scientific method and data presentation.*

O Solving Behavior Problems in Autism. Hodgdon, Linda. (1999). Michigan: Quirk Roberts
Publishing.
*This book is an excellent addition to the previous resource book Visual Strategies for Improving
Communication. This edition provides educators, and parents alike with specific problem situa-
tions that can be effectively managed with visual supports in the classroom, home and commu-
nity. This book is especially helpful in working with larger populations, not just young children.
The suggestions are useful for behavior management from early intervention through adulthood.*

O Teaching Children with Autism: Strategies to Enhance Communication and Socialization.
Quill, Kathleen. (1995). Albany, New York: Delmar Publishers, Inc.
*This book is very useful and full of practical ideas accompanied by vignettes of teachers who
work with children with autism. Thoughtful writings explore cognition, social interaction and
communication with their unique connection to the autism diagnosis. Throughout the book, there
are techniques and strategies, but all respect the fact that these are children first, with autism
second. The strategies given are easily used in daily living activities, which create a natural
approach to intervention.*

O Teaching Children with Autism: Strategies for Initiating Positive Interactions and
Improving Learning Opportunities. Koegel R.L. & Koegel L.K. (1995). Maryland: Paul H.
Brookes Publishing.
*The chapters in this book focus on the goals of intervention. This book is especially helpful for
individuals that are putting together an educational plan for a child with autism, and parents
that are deciding what supports are necessary for their child.*

O The Pretenders: Gifted People Who Have Difficulty Learning. Guyer, Barbara. (1997).
*This book is for educators, parents and professionals working directly with students with special
needs. It is a collection of several anecdotal case studies of students referred to a special educa-
tion/learning disabilities clinic in a North Carolina college campus. It recounts the emotional and
personal stories of several adults with various learning disabilities who are very intelligent and
learn to overcome their learning disability and develop greater self-esteem as well as become
highly successful professionals in their respective fields.*

O Thinking in Pictures and Other Reports from My Life with Autism. Grandin, T. (1995).
New York: Vintage Books.
*This book was very insightful and full of detailed knowledge about autism. Ms. Grandin writes
very straightforwardly about her life with autism and her accomplishments (which are many)
that she feels are directly related to her unique perspective in life. Also full of research regarding
medical interventions, history, various perspectives from other individuals with autism, and the
latest research regarding treatment and theories about autism, this book is a must read for
anyone working with children or adults with autism, as it is a valuable informational resource as*

well as a wonderful autobiographical work that provides an unparalleled look at life with autism.

o   The World of the Autistic Child: Understanding and Treating Autistic Spectrum Disorders.
Siegel, B. (1996). New York: Oxford University Press.
This book gives the reader a comprehensive step by step look at the process of treating the disorder. It guides you through defining the diagnosis based on DSM-IV-R criteria, social development of a child diagnosed, focusing on peer interaction and language. This book also includes a section on family support and coping strategies with a extensive section on treatment resources.

o   When Autism Strikes: Families Cope with Childhood Disintegrative Disorder. Catalano,
R.A. Ed. (1998). New York: Plenum Press.
This is a very touching book that gives families stories of the emotional trials and tribulations that encompass dealing with a child that has Childhood Disintegrative Disorder. It is a useful tool for parents learning to cope and work through the grief of this devastating trauma.

o   Visual Strategies for Improving Communication, Volume 1. Hodgdon, Linda. (1998).
Michigan: Quirk Roberts Publishing. This book is for educators. It provides practical ideas for organizing, implementing and maintaining a visual communication system in home, school and community environments. It gives many examples of specific strategies and techniques to begin a visual communication system and to maintain effectiveness with progress.

Internet sites:

o   Autism Society of America, www.autism-society.org

o   ASAT –Association for Science in Autism, www.asatonline.org

o   Report of the Recommendations of the Clinical Practice Guidelines on Autism/Pervasive
Development Disorders/Evaluation, Assessment, NY State Dept. of Health,
www.health.state.ny.us

o   PECS, The Picture Exchange Communication System, www.pecs.com; This website will
provide all the information needed about the manual, videos and supplies for this visual
system.

o   Social skills and language pragmatics- NLD Line; www.nldline.com

o   A good resource for parents, including an article on the Teacher's role in developing
social skills can be found at www.kidsource.com

o   A site to find information on Young's Children's Social Development, including the Eric
Digest on the Social Attributes Checklist can be found at www.ed.gov/databases/eric-
digest

○ A neat concept for setting up visual-based guides for teaching beginning play skills can be found at www.playsteps.com

○ ERIC Clearinghouse on Disabilities and Gifted Education (ERIC EC) The largest database of education-related documents, journal citations, and other print materials. http://www.cec.sped.org.ericec.htm

○ Language Pathologists and related fields, www.gift-inc.com

○ **The Center for Effective Collaboration and Practice**
An IEP Team's Introduction To Functional Behavioral Assessment and Behavior Intervention Plans (2nd edition)
www.air-dc.org/cecp/resources/problembehavior/main.htm

○ **Utah's BEST Project**
A statewide project focused on bringing effective behavioral strategies into the classroom
http://www.usoe.k12.ut.us/sars/best/deb.html

○ **Syracuse City School District**
Behavior Consultation Team and School-based Intervention Teams Program
http://www.scsd.k12.ny.us/sbit/dirhtml/bctfile/bctdrpg.html

○ **New York Autism Network**
Provides information on training activities across the state, fact sheets on educating students with autism and related disorders, and links to other organizations
http://www.albany.edu/psy/autism/autism.html

○ **The Beach Center**
Sample newsletters, advocacy how-to's, fellowship opportunities for parents, coping strategies for a disability diagnosis, laws that affect families, links to other sites.
http://www.lsi.ukans.edu/beach/beachhp.htm

○ **National Information Center for Children and Youth with Disabilities (NICHCY)**
Information and referral center that provides information on disabilities and disability-related issues
http://www.nichcy.org

○ A great website to find lots of information and links about autism can be found on the award-winning website by the center for the study of autism: www.autism.org

○ Information and articles on social skills can be found at the FEAT website, by logging on to www.feat.org/autism/social_skill.htm

○ An interesting source of learning materials can be found at this website: Home schooling

203

kids at www.members.tripod.com

○ A good website to find different ways to order visuals to help teach with and to help schedule with, along with computer software can be found at www.do2learn.com or at www.usevisualstrategies.com

○ A fun website filled with jokes for kids can be found at www.scatty.com

○ A cute book on using video modeling to teach and written by a mom, can be found at www.ideasaboutautism.com

○ The idiom connection can be found at www.geocities.com

○ Pen pals via email for kids with disabilities can be found at www.ebuddies.org

○ Surfer's Healing surf camp for children with autism, www.surfershealing.org

○ Find out about Kelly McKinnon and Janis Krempa at www.kellymckinnon.com

○ Different Roads To Learning, www.difflearn.com, has a great website and catalog and is a complete ABA resource.

VHS/DVD's
* viewed, but not able to accurately reference because of lack of complete bibliography information:

○ Watch Me Learn. 2004, Marybeth Palo. Available at www.difflearn.com

○ Fitting In, Having Fun. 2004, TD Scial Skills. www.tdsocialskills.com

○ PBS Video series: Oliver Sacks: Autism. PBS Video. 1-800-328-PBS1, Alexandria, VA.

○ The Autism Partnership, Boston Chapter. 1997. Bridget Taylor. Teaching initiation skills to children with autism.

○ The Autism Partnership, Boston Chapter. 1998. Elizabeth Steege. Play skills and children with autism.

○ The Autism Partnership, Boston Chapter. 1998. Dr. Gina Green. Generalization strategies for children with autism.

○ The Alpine Learning Center. 1999. Dr. Bridget Taylor. Transferring a child's appropriate behavior from classroom to community settings.

○ Greater Washington Educational Television Association. 1994. Dr. Richard Lavoie. Last one picked, first one picked on. PBS Video. 1-800-328-PBS1, Alexandria, VA.

Assessment Tools

○ **Help Strands Assessment & Curriculum Guide**
Vort Corporation P.O. Box 60132 Palo Alto, CA 94306

○ **Social Behavior Assessment Inventory**
Psychological Assessment Resources, Inc. P.O. Box 998/Odessa, Fl. 33556

○ **Scales for Predicting Successful Inclusion** (SPSI)
James E. Gillan, Kathleen S. McConell, Pro-ed Publishing

○ **Vineland Adaptive Behavior Scales**
American Guidance Service, Inc., 4201 Woodland Road, Circle Pines, MN 55014

BIBLIOGRAPHY

Functional Assessment

Broussard, C., & Northrup, J. (1995). An approach to functional assessment and analysis of disruptive behavior in regular education classrooms. **School Psychology Quarterly**, 10, 151-164.

Daly, E., Witt, J., Martens, B., & Dool, E. (1997). A model for conducting a functional analysis of academic performance problems. **School Psychology Review**, 26, 554-574.

Demchak, M. (1993). Functional assessment of problem behaviors in applied settings. **Intervention in School and Clinic**, 29, 89-95.

Derby, K.M., Wacker, D.P., Peck, S., Sasso, G., DeRaad, A., Berg, W., Asmus, J., & Ulrich, S. (1994). Functional analysis of separate topographies of aberrant behavior. **Journal of Applied Behavior Analysis**, 27, 267-278.

Dunlap, G., & Kern, L. (1993). Assessment and intervention for children within the instructional curriculum. In J. Reichle & D. Wacker (Eds.), **Communicative approaches to the management of challenging behaviors**, (pp. 135-173). Baltimore: Paul H. Brookes.

Dunlap, G., Kern-Dunlap, L., Clarke, S., & Robbins, F.R. (1991). Functional assessment, curricular revision, and severe behavior problems. **Journal of Applied Behavioral Analysis**, 24, 387-397.

Durand, V.M., & Crimmins, D.B. (1988). Identifying the variables maintaining self-injurious behavior. **Journal of Autism and Developmental Disorders**, 18, 99-117.

Durand, V.M., & Crimmins, D.B. (1992). **The Motivation Assessment Scale administration guide**. Topeka, KS: Monaco & Associates.

Durand, V.M., Crimmins, D.B., Caulfield, M., & Taylor, J. (1989). Reinforcer assessment I: Using problem behaviors to select reinforcers. **Journal of the Association for Persons with Severe Handicaps**, 14, 113-126.

Ervin, R.A., DuPaul, G.J., Kern, L., & Friman, P.C. (1998). Classroom-based functional and adjunctive assessments: Proactive approaches to intervention selection for adolescents with attention deficit hyperactivity disorder. **Journal of Applied Behavior Analysis**, 31, 65-78.

Fisher, W.W., Adelinis, J.D., Thompson, R.H., Wordsell, A.S., & Zarcone, J.R. (1988). Functional analysis and treatment of destructive behavior maintained by termination of "don't" (and symmetrical "do") requests. **Journal of Applied Behavior Analysis**, 31, 339-356.

Foster-Johnson, L., Dunlap, G. (1993). Using functional assessment to develop effective individualized interventions for challenging behaviors. **Teaching Exceptional Children**, 25, 44-50.

Fowler, R.C., & Schnacker, L.E. (1994). The changing character of behavioral assessment and treatment: An historical introduction and review of functional analysis research. **Diagnostique**, 19, 79-102.

Gable, R.A. (1996). A critical analysis of functional assessment: Issues for researchers and practitioners. **Behavioral Disorders**, 22, 36-40.

Groden, G. (1989). A guide for conducting a comprehensive behavioral analysis of a target behavior. **Journal of Behavior Therapy and Experimental Psychiatry**, 20, 163-169.

Hendrikson, J.M., Gable, R.A., Novak, C., & Peck, S. (1996). Functional assessment as strategy assessment for teaching academics. **Education and Treatment of Children**, 19, 257-271.

Iwata, B.A., Dorsey, M.F., Slifer, K.J., Bauman, K.E., & Richman, G.S. (1982). Toward a functional analysis of self-injury. **Analysis and Intervention in Developmental Disabilities**, 2, 3-20.

Lalli, J.S., & Kates, K. (1998). The effect of reinforcer preference on functional analysis outcomes. **Journal of Applied Behavior Analysis**, 31, 79-90.

Lohrmann-O'Rourke, S., Knoster, T., & Llewellyn, G. (1999). Screening for understanding. **Journal of Positive Behavior Interventions**, 1, 35-42.

O'Neill, R. E., Horner, R.H., Albin, R.W., Sprague, J.R., Storey, K., Newton, J.S. (1997). **Functional assessment and program development for problem behavior**. Pacific Grove, CA: Brookes/Cole.

Steege, M., & Northrup, T. (1998). Brief functional analysis of problem behavior: A practical approach of school psychologists. **Proven Practice**, 1, 4-11 and 37-38.

PBS Planning and Applications

Crimmins, D.B., & Woolf, S.B. (1997). **Positive Strategies: Training teams in positive behavior support**. Valhalla, NY: Westchester Institute for Human Development.

Davis, C.A., & Reichle, J. (1996). Variant and invariant high-probability requests: Increasing appropriate behaviors in children with emotional-behavioral disorders. **Journal of Applied Behavior Analysis**, 29, 471-482.

Dunlap, G., dePerczel, M., Clarke, S., Wilson, D., Wright, S., White, R., & Gomez, A. (1994). Choice making to promote adaptive behavior for students with emotional and behavioral challenges. **Journal of Applied Behavioral Analysis**, 27, 505-518.

Durand, V.M. (1990). **Severe behavior problems: A functional communication training approach**. New York: Guilford Press.

Durand, V.M., & Crimmins, D.B. (1991). Teaching functionally equivalent responses as an intervention for challenging behavior. In B. Remington (Ed.), **The challenge of severe mental handicap: A behavior analytic approach**. Chi Chester, England: John Wiley & Sons Ltd.

Foster-Johnson, L., Ferro, J., & Dunlap, G. (1994). Preferred curricular activities and reduced problem behaviors in students with intellectual disabilities. **Journal of Applied Behavior Analysis**, 27, 493-504.

Goldstein, A. (1988). **The PREPARE Curriculum**. Champaign, IL: Research Press.

Goldstein, A., & McGinnis, E.M. (1997). **Skillstreaming the adolescent: New strategies and perspectives for teaching prosocial skills**. Champaign, IL: Research Press.

Hedeen, D.L., Ayres, B.J., Meyer, L.H., & Waite, J. (1996). Quality inclusive schooling for students with severe behavioral challenges. In D. Lehr and F. Brown (Eds.). **People with disabilities who challenge the system**. Baltimore: Paul H. Brookes Publishing Co.

Horner, R.H., Carr, E.G. (1997). Behavioral support for students with severe disabilities: Functional assessment and comprehensive intervention. **Journal of Special Education**, 31, 84-104.

Horner, R.H., Dunlap, G., Koegel, R.L., Carr, E.G., Sailor, W., Anderson, J. Albin, R.W., & O=Neill, R.E. (1987). Toward a technology of "nonaversive@ behavioral support. **Journal of the Association for Persons with Severe Handicaps**, 12, 18-27.

Kern, L., Childs, K.E., Dunlap, G., Clarke, Shelley, & Falk, G.D. (1994). Using assessment-based curricular intervention to improve the classroom behavior of a student with emotional and behavioral challenges. **Journal of Applied Behavior Analysis**, 27, 7-19.

Koegel, L.K., Harrower, J.K., & Koegel, R.L. (1999). Support for children with developmental disabilities in full inclusion classrooms through self-management. **Journal of Positive Behavior Interventions**, 1, 26-34.

Koegel, L.K., Koegel, R.L., & Dunlap, G. (Eds.). (1996). **Positive behavioral support: Including people with difficult behavior in the community**. Baltimore: Paul H. Brookes Publishing Co.

Lehr, D. & Brown, F. (1996). **People with disabilities who challenge the system**. Baltimore: Paul H. Brookes Publishing Co.

McGinnis, E.M., & Goldstein, A. (1997). **Skillstreaming the elementary school child:**

New strategies and perspectives for teaching prosocial skills. Champaign, IL: Research Press.

Meyer, L.H., & Evans, I.M. (1989). **Nonaversive intervention for behavior problems**. Baltimore: Paul H. Brookes Publishing Co.

Smith, R.G., & Iwata, B.A. (1997). Antecedent influences on behavior disorders. **Journal of Applied Behavior Analysis**, 30, 343-375.

Todd, A., Horner, R., Sugai, G., Sprague, J.R. (in press). Effective behavior support: Strengthening school-wide systems through a team based approach. **Effective School Practices**. Association of Direct Instruction.

Vollmer, T.R., Iwata, B.A., Zarcone, J.R., Smith, R.G., & Mazaleski, J.L. (1993). The role of attention in the treatment of attention-maintained self-injurious behavior: Noncontingent reinforcement and differential reinforcement of other behavior. **Journal of Applied Behavior Analysis**, 26, 9-21.

Walker, H.M., Colvin, G., & Ramsey, E. (1995). **Antisocial behavior in school: Strategies and best practices**. Pacific Grove, CA: Brookes/Cole.

Barnhill, Gena P., Cook, Tapscott Katherine, Tebbenkamp, Cook & Myles, Brenda Smith (2002) The effectiveness of Social Skill Intervention Targeting Nonverbal Communication for Adolescents with Asperger's Syndrome and Related Pervasive Developmental Delays. **Focus on Autism and Other Developmental Disabilities**, Volume 17, Number 2, Summer 2002, pages 112-118.

Terpstra, Judith E., Higgins, Kyle, Pierce , Tom (2002) Can I play? Classroom-based Interventions for Teaching Play Skills to Children with Autism. **Focus on Autism and Other Developmental Disabilities**, Volume 17, Number 2, Summer 2002, pages 119-126